Ellen Ochoa

TITLES IN THE
LATINO BIOGRAPHY LIBRARY SERIES:

César Chávez
A Voice for
Farmworkers

ISBN-13: 978-0-7660-2489-2
ISBN-10: 0-7660-2489-X

Diego Rivera
Legendary
Mexican Painter

ISBN-13: 978-0-7660-2486-1
ISBN-10: 0-7660-2486-5

Freddie Prinze, Jr.
From Shy Guy to
Movie Star

ISBN-13: 978-0-7660-2965-1
ISBN-10: 0-7660-2965-4

Frida Kahlo
Her Life in
Paintings

ISBN-13: 978-0-7660-2487-8
ISBN-10: 0-7660-2487-3

George Lopez
Latino King of
Comedy

ISBN-13: 978-0-7660-2968-2
ISBN-10: 0-7660-2968-9

Gloria Estefan
Superstar of
Song

ISBN-13: 978-0-7660-2490-8
ISBN-10: 0-7660-2490-3

Isabel Allende
Award-Winning
Latin American
Author

ISBN-13: 978-0-7660-2488-5
ISBN-10: 0-7660-2488-1

Pablo Neruda
Passion, Poetry,
Politics

ISBN-13: 978-0-7660-2966-8
ISBN-10: 0-7660-2966-2

Jaime Escalante
Inspirational Math
Teacher

ISBN-13: 978-0-7660-2967-5
ISBN-10: 0-7660-2967-0

Roberto Clemente
Baseball Legend

ISBN-13: 978-0-7660-2485-4
ISBN-10: 0-7660-2485-7

LATINO BIOGRAPHY LIBRARY

Ellen Ochoa

Astronaut and Inventor

ANNE SCHRAFF

Enslow Publishers, Inc.
40 Industrial Road
Box 398
Berkeley Heights, NJ 07922
USA

http://www.enslow.com

Library of Congress Cataloging-in-Publication Data:

Schraff, Anne E.
 Ellen Ochoa : astronaut and inventor / Anne Schraff.
   p. cm. — (Latino biography library)
 Includes bibliographical references and index.
 Summary: "Explores the life of Ellen Ochoa, including her childhood in California, her rise through the ranks in NASA, several space shuttle missions, and becoming the first Latino woman in space"—Provided by publisher.
 ISBN-13: 978-0-7660-3163-0
 ISBN-10: 0-7660-3163-2
 1. Ochoa, Ellen—Juvenile literature. 2. Astronauts—United States—Biography—Juvenile litera-ture. 3. Inventors—United States—Biography—Juvenile literature. 4. Women astronauts—United States—Biography—Juvenile literature. 5. Women inventors—United States—Biography—Juvenile literature. 6. Hispanic Americans—Biography—Juvenile literature. I. Title.
 TL789.85.O25S37 2010
 629.450092—dc22
 [B]
                                        2008040349

Printed in the United States of America

10 9 8 7 6 5 4 3 2 1

To Our Readers:
We have done our best to make sure all Internet Addresses in this book were active and appro-priate when we went to press. However, the author and the publisher have no control over and assume no liability for the material available on those Internet sites or on other Web sites they may link to. Any comments or suggestions can be sent by e-mail to comments@enslow.com or to the address on the back cover.

Illustration Credits: Associated Press, p. 47; Great Images in NASA (NASA-HQ-GRIN), pp. 55, 67; Grossmont High School (photo by Boyd Anderson), p. 24; Hugh Threlfall/Alamy, p. 100; Jack Smith/Bloomberg News/Landov, pp. 16–17; National Aeronautics and Space Administration (NASA), pp. 3, 89, 93, 97; National Aeronautics and Space Administration (NASA)/Bill Ingalls, p. 110; National Aeronautics and Space Administration, Johnson Space Center (NASA-JSC), pp. 5, 6, 8–9, 12–13, 44–45, 48–49, 58, 61, 62, 70, 74, 77; National Aeronautics and Space Administration, Kennedy Space Center (NASA-KSC), pp. 37, 82, 85, 87; National Aeronautics and Space Administration, Marshall Space Flight Center (NASA-MSFC), pp. 20, 30, 81; Reuters/Landov, p. 104; Sandia National Lab, p. 35; San Diego State University, p. 26.

Cover Illustration: National Aeronautics and Space Administration (NASA)
(Ochoa in an orange space suit).

Contents

Official NASA portrait of Ellen Ochoa, Ph.D. Ochoa wears a navy blue flight suit with a space shuttle model displayed on her left.

1

Space Adventure

The space shuttle *Discovery* sped through space. It was Day Four of the nine-day mission to study the atmosphere of earth. Rookie astronaut Ellen Ochoa was in space for the first time. She had a very difficult job ahead. The success of the mission depended on how well she did her job.

Ochoa would use a 50-foot-long robot arm RMS (remote manipulator system) to lift a 2,800-pound (1,270-kilogram) satellite from the cargo bay of the shuttle. Then the RMS would send the satellite into space. The satellite, named *Spartan,* was a bright, gold-colored object about the size of an air conditioner. Inside *Spartan* were two telescopes. They would study the fiery halo around the sun called the corona.

Ellen Ochoa used the robot arm to gently lift *Spartan.* "She did it very carefully, very slowly," Program Manager Montoya said. "It was a gem."[1] Ochoa sent *Spartan* toward the sun. "Sure was pretty to see that thing go," said *Discovery* commander Kenneth Cameron.[2]

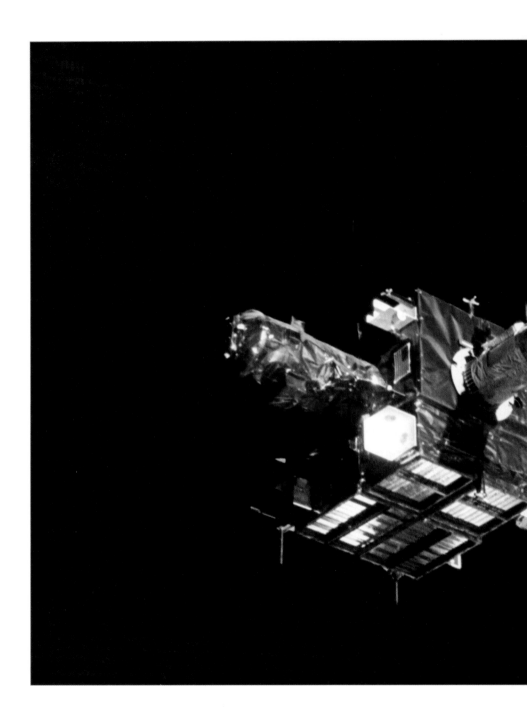

The STS-56 remote manipulator system grapples for the Shuttle Pointed Autonomous Research Tool for Astronomy 201 (SPARTAN-201) on April 17, 1993.

The National Aeronautics and Space Administration (NASA) said the launch of *Spartan* was "just perfect, right on the timeline."[3] Ellen Ochoa had passed her first big test. She came through with flying colors. But she was far from done. In two days, she would have to use the RMS again to pull *Spartan* back into the space shuttle's cargo bay.

Spartan measured the atmosphere around the sun for two days. All the information was stored inside *Spartan*. If the satellite were not recovered, it would all be lost.

On Tuesday, the day *Spartan* was to be recovered, everybody was focused. The space shuttle was speeding through space. The shuttle and satellite were both far above the South Pacific as Ellen Ochoa got ready to pluck *Spartan* from space. Commander Ken Cameron

Space Shuttle

The space shuttle is a reusable spacecraft. It is launched into space. After the mission, it reenters the earth's atmosphere. It can fly and land like an airplane. The space shuttle has four main parts. The orbiter, which looks like an airplane, is where the crew lives and works. It also has a large outside fuel tank and two rockets. During liftoff the rockets boost the space shuttle into orbit. Then the rockets fall into the ocean. They can be recovered, cleaned, and then used again. Once the main engines shut down, the fuel tank separates from the orbiter and breaks up as it falls through the atmosphere. But the orbiter lands and will fly again on the next mission.

> *"It is a very beautiful sight. You can see cities, mountain ranges, lakes. We never got tired of looking at it."*[4] –Ellen Ochoa describing the view from the space shuttle.

moved *Discovery* closer and closer to *Spartan*. Finally the two spacecrafts were just thirty-five feet apart. Ochoa was operating the robot arm skillfully. She nudged *Spartan* toward the cargo bay of the space shuttle.

Back at Mission Control in Houston, Texas, NASA officials watched anxiously. If *Spartan* drifted away and out of reach, it would cost NASA much valuable data as well as a valuable piece of equipment. Ochoa used all the training she had received to capture *Spartan* and then prepare to berth it. Finally, *Spartan* slipped into the cargo bay.

"Great work, Ellen," Mission Control at NASA said. "There are a lot of smiles in the room down here. Congratulations on a fantastic rendezvous and grapple."[5]

With *Spartan* safely in the cargo bay, Ochoa described her first experience in space as a "real interesting ride. A lot different than anything else that I've ever done before."[6] For the thirty-four-year old Latina astronaut it was just the beginning of many space adventures.

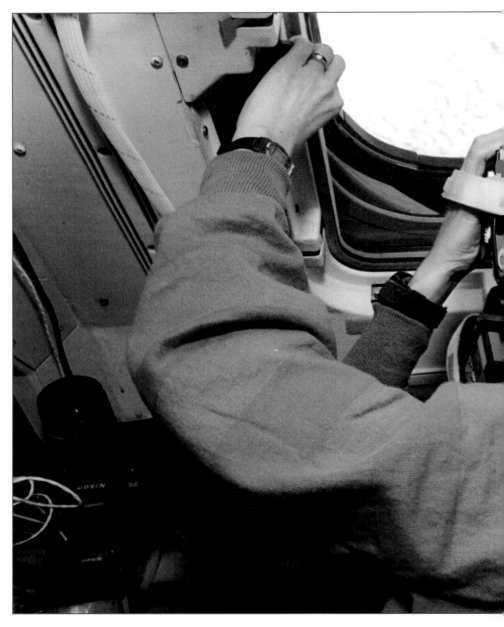

Ellen Ochoa points a camera out an overhead window on the aft flight deck of the *Discovery*.

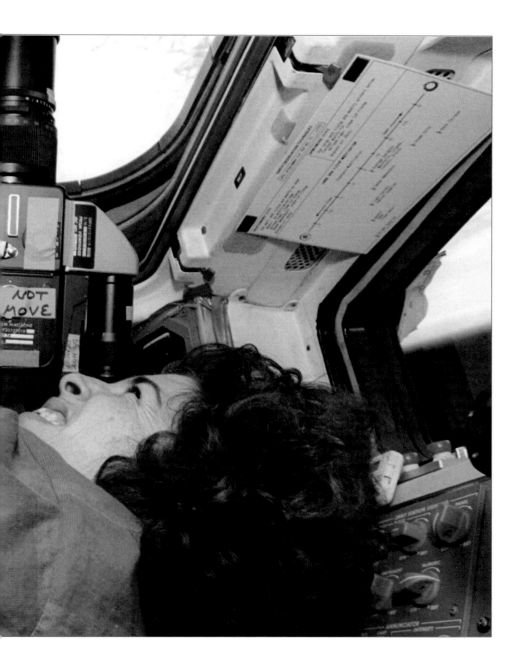

2

California Childhood

Ellen Lauri Ochoa was born in Los Angeles, California, on May 10, 1958. She was the third in a family of five children. Ellen's mother was Rosanne Deardorff, who was born in Tulsa, Oklahoma, in 1920. As a small child, Rosanne had such severe asthma (a disorder that causes difficulty in breathing and fits of coughing) that she could not go to school. Asthma can be related to climate, so her parents decided to move to California. Rosanne, her mother, and her sister Gloria arrived in Hollywood, California. Rosanne's asthma was better, but she was still unable to go to school. As a result, she was privately tutored at home.

When she was a teenager, Rosanne became an usher at Grauman's Chinese Theatre in Hollywood. This was a very famous movie theatre. Movie stars appeared there often. Rosanne and her sister met many well-known movie stars. They had their pictures taken with actors like Clark Gable and child star Shirley Temple. Later, Ellen Ochoa said her mother and her aunt were "big movie fans."[1] Later, Rosanne became a secretary to the head of a movie studio.

Ellen's father was Joseph Ochoa, who was born in California, one of twelve children. His parents had moved to Arizona and then California from Sonora, a large Mexican state with mountains and deserts. They were looking for a better life for their family.

Joseph Ochoa's father was a newspaper editor in Mexico and a store owner in California. Ellen Ochoa never knew her grandfather, but she was thirteen when her grandmother died at the age of ninety-three.

Joseph Ochoa grew up in a bilingual home (where both Spanish and English were spoken). The family spoke mostly Spanish, but Ochoa decided that when he had his own family they would speak English.

Ochoa and his brothers and sisters had some painful experiences growing up. For example, Hispanic children were not allowed to use the city's public pool except for

La Mesa, California

La Mesa is about ten miles east of San Diego, California. It was founded in 1869 and was incorporated as a town in 1912. In the early 1900s, it was known as the movie capital of the West. One hundred short westerns and comedies were made there. Then the movie business moved to Hollywood. La Mesa in Spanish means "the table" or "the plateau." It has many tree-lined streets and hills. The nickname for La Mesa is the Jewel of the Hills.

one day a week, the day before the pool received its weekly cleaning.

Years later, when Ellen Ochoa was an adult, she said she was sorry she had not learned to speak Spanish as a child. She was sad that she had not learned much of her father's Mexican heritage. But she understood her father's attitude. He was eager for his children to be successful and wanted them to be fluent in English.

World War II ended in 1945. Joseph Ochoa graduated from the U.S. Naval Academy the same year and served in the navy at the very end of the war. He

Homes under construction in La Mesa, California, in October 2007.

remained in the navy for a while after coming home. He had met Rosanne Deardorff in high school and they had fallen in love. Joseph Ochoa and Rosanne Deardorff were married in Los Angeles in 1946. After leaving the navy in 1947, Ochoa found a job with Sears Roebuck, a large department store and mail-order house. Soon the Ochoas welcomed a daughter, Beth, and a son, Monte. Ellen Ochoa was born in 1958.

When Ellen was one year old, her father was transferred to San Diego. He would be superintendent of the Sears Roebuck store there. It was a good promotion with

extra money for a growing family. The Ochoas found a house in La Mesa, a suburb of San Diego.

With Ellen just a year old, and Beth and Monte still small children, Rosanne Ochoa, a strong believer in education, enrolled in San Diego State University. She took just one or two courses each semester while she raised her children.

The Ochoa family added two more sons after the move to La Mesa. First came Tyler, and then the last, Wilson. The family now had five children. The Ochoa children were all good students. They studied and took part in many other activities. Ellen became interested in music at an early age. She enjoyed playing the flute.

Rosanne Ochoa was busy every day taking her children to and from their different after-school activities. They had band practice, junior theatre, and sports. Also, Rosanne Ochoa was president of the Parent-Teacher Association (PTA) at Northmont Elementary School, where her children attended classes. She also volunteered at nearby Grossmont Hospital.

Ellen Ochoa was an eager reader as a child. She was especially interested in books about fantastic worlds. She read *The Hobbit* by J.R.R. Tolkien. She was delighted by the strange creatures. But her all-time favorite was *A Wrinkle in Time* by Madeleine L'Engle. In this book a little girl named Meg and her friends travel across space on a rescue

> *"My first priority was raising my family and school came second. I don't regret taking that long at all."[2] Sixty-two-year-old Rosanne Ochoa talking about receiving her college degree. It had taken her twenty-two years.*

mission. Ellen enjoyed reading the adventures of daring Meg, and her spirit remained in the back of Ellen's imagination. The book had planted seeds that would someday blossom into real-life adventures for Ellen.

In the early 1960s, both the United States and the Soviet Union had space programs. The rivalry called the Cold War between the United States and the Soviet Union spilled over into the space race. When the Soviet Union put Yuri Gagarin into orbital flight in April 1961, the first human in space, Americans were determined to match and surpass their rival. In May 1961, when Ellen Ochoa was three years old, American astronaut Alan B. Shepard, Jr., went into space. In 1962, John Glenn became the first American to orbit earth. All during the 1960s, Americans and Russians were circling the earth in spacecrafts. Like all the children of that time, Ellen watched the television news programs with stories about the newest space adventures. It was exciting to her, but she never imagined she might someday be a part of it. Later she said, "Women weren't accepted into the astronaut corps until I was halfway through college, so I hadn't considered it as a career when I was young."[3]

Ellen was an excellent student at Northmont Elementary School in La Mesa. All of the Ochoa children were bright students with high energy. Ellen continued to excel at Parkway Junior High, also in La Mesa. At age thirteen she won the San Diego Spelling Bee. She also earned the honor of Outstanding Seventh and Eighth Grade Student at Parkway.

Alan B. Shepard was the first American in space. His flight launched on May 5, 1961, and it lasted fifteen minutes.

When Ellen was twelve years old, a dramatic change occurred in the family. Joseph Ochoa, her father, moved away. Rosanne and Joseph later divorced. That left the major responsibility of caring for the family to Ellen's mother.

Ellen Ochoa later recalled her mother's devotion to the family. She remembered periods when her mother was taking her five children to twelve music lessons a week. Whatever the children were inspired to do, their mother was eager to help give them the chance. "She devoted most of her life to raising her children and remained their strongest supporter throughout her life," Ellen Ochoa said of her mother.[4]

Rosanne Ochoa not only used words to inspire her children, but she taught them by the example of her own life. Ellen and her sister and brothers watched their mother come home from her own college classes, filled with excitement. A student at San Diego State University, Rosanne Ochoa shared events from her classes. She was enthusiastic about every new thing she learned. It was a powerful lesson for her children. It taught them that learning was not a boring duty. It was thrilling.

In addition to being a good student as a child, Ellen was also a talented musician and a good athlete. At that young age, however, she did not show great interest in science. This came much later.

It would be a very long time before Ellen's dreams would extend to space.

3

Education

In 1971, Ellen Ochoa became a student at Grossmont High School in La Mesa. Before thirteen-year-old Ellen began her high school studies, the United States space program had accomplished amazing things. After the first landing on the moon on July 20, 1969, there were more lunar journeys. Three American astronauts, led by Alan Shepard, made the third moon landing in January 1971. In July 1971 the fourth moon landing used the lunar rover to drive around the moon's surface. Around the time Ellen started her sophomore year at Grossmont High, the fifth moon landing took place.

At this time of her life, Ellen had no idea she would one day be part of the space program. She had not yet even focused on math and science. She liked so many different subjects that she was not ready to focus on just one area. In fact, Ellen really liked American and English literature. She later recalled that she was "drawn to teachers who made class interesting."[1] She mentioned two Grossmont High teachers who did just that: Jeanne

Dorsey and Dani Barton. They made their classes come alive and their students want to learn.

Ellen continued to play the flute and became more accomplished. She loved the instrument and practiced as often as she could. She was skilled enough to become a member of the Civic Youth Orchestra in San Diego, as a classical flutist. She was still hoping to become a classical musician.

Grossmont High had excellent math and science classes, but teachers did not encourage girls to take them. As a result, most of these classes were filled with boys. But Ellen Ochoa was fortunate to have a female calculus teacher—Paz Jensen—who made her feel very welcome in class. Ellen later recalled how Jensen made math "appealing and motivated me to continue studying it."[2] Because of this encouragement she would take other advanced math classes. The fact that Ellen enrolled in that calculus class with Jensen showed a willingness to explore an area that was dominated by boys.

Ellen was recognized as the best math student in her class. When she graduated from Grossmont High in

The Flute

The flute is a woodwind instrument. It is like a hollow pipe with holes along its length. It has been used since ancient times. In Asia, flute players often used bamboo tubes. Now, flutes are usually made from silver. The flute makes a clear, soft sound that is very beautiful.

Ellen Ochoa's high school yearbook portrait. Her nickname in high school was "E."

1975, she was valedictorian. This is an honor given to the high school student with the best grades.

Ellen Ochoa was offered a four-year scholarship to Stanford University. Stanford is a large school in northern California with a great reputation. Ellen knew that attending Stanford would be a great asset to her future. However, even with the scholarship, there were additional expenses that the family could not afford. Joseph Ochoa would not be contributing and Rosanne Ochoa still had two younger children at home, teenagers Tyler and Wilson. Ellen had just turned seventeen, and her mother felt she was too young to leave home and attend school in northern California. So Ellen turned down the Stanford scholarship and instead enrolled at nearby San Diego State University. She would live at home while pursuing her studies, and she would help her mother with her two younger brothers.

Seventeen-year-old Ellen Ochoa joined the freshman class at San Diego State in 1975. At about this time, NASA was changing the direction of the space program. Everything NASA had sent into space before then could be used just once. That was costly. NASA engineers wondered, could they build a winged aircraft that went into space and then returned? The engineers started to design what would become the space shuttle.

Ellen Ochoa had no firm plans yet about what she would major in at San Diego State. A musical career still appealed to her. She could imagine herself as part of a symphony orchestra. She loved to make beautiful music. She was also interested in journalism. Perhaps she would become a reporter. The problem was that she enjoyed so many things and was good at them, so it was hard to settle on one goal.

Ellen Ochoa changed her major five times at San Diego State. She found that she really enjoyed physics

Ochoa in the physics lab at San Diego State University.

and she thought seriously about an engineering career. With this in mind, she discussed her future with a professor at San Diego State. He told her that engineering would be too difficult a field for a woman. He said it was a man's world. So Ellen Ochoa took physics and studied matter and energy.

At the time Ellen Ochoa was studying at San Diego State, her siblings Beth and Monte were also students there. Rosanne Ochoa was also continuing her long journey toward a degree. Rosanne Ochoa was fifty-five when Ellen enrolled at San Diego State. She had been working on her college degree for sixteen years, since she was thirty-nine years old. At that time she was taking biology, business, and journalism. As her children grew older and

> *"I did not have a single woman science or engineering professor my entire ten years in college. In many cases I was the only female student in the class as well."[3] Ellen Ochoa commenting on the lack of female role models for girls in the scientific field.*

needed her less, she was able to take more classes each semester. Her dream was in sight. Although four members of the Ochoa family attended San Diego State at the same time, they never had a class together. There were more than thirty thousand students at the college, and their paths never crossed.

In 1978, something happened in the space program that got Ellen Ochoa's attention. NASA graduated the first six women ever selected for the astronaut program. Ochoa later recalled thinking, "Oh, it's really open to real people, not just an elite group of test pilots."[4]

In June 1980, Ellen Ochoa graduated from San Diego State University. She had a Bachelor of Science (BS) degree in physics. Ochoa graduated with high honors. She was again valedictorian with a perfect grade point average of 4.0. Ochoa was one of the few students ever to receive an A in Professor Morris's physics laboratory.

After graduating from San Diego State University, Ellen Ochoa was still undecided about her future. She had not yet ruled out a musical career. She also considered using her mathematical skills in the business world.

Rosanne Ochoa played a big role in the decision Ellen Ochoa finally made. Rosanne Ochoa was very grateful for the sacrifice her daughter had made in turning down the Stanford scholarship four years earlier so she could help with the children still at home. But the younger Ochoa boys were now grown and away at college themselves. Rosanne Ochoa told her daughter it was time to go to Stanford as a graduate student. Ellen

Stanford University

Stanford University is located in northern California near Palo Alto. It was founded by Leland Stanford, railroad man, governor, and senator from California. Stanford has a medical center, a marine biology unit, and eleven overseas study centers. It is highly respected as a center of research.

Ochoa would be able to gain the fine education Stanford offered after all.

So Ellen Ochoa enrolled at Stanford at age twenty-two. She was excited about going there. She liked the fact that Stanford offered many classes in the humanities—history, literature, and music. Ochoa did not want to just take math and science classes.

As Ellen Ochoa headed for Stanford in the fall of 1980, NASA's plans for a reusable spacecraft were moving ahead. A test version of the craft had been built. The space shuttle *Enterprise* was being tested in flight. The main problem was in the ceramic tiles on the outside of the *Enterprise*. During actual launches, the temperatures would be very high and the ceramic tiles would provide protection. Unfortunately, they kept falling off during the tests. The *Enterprise* would never go into space. But another space shuttle, *Columbia*, was getting ready for flight. Engineers worked on the ceramic tile problem, which had to be solved before *Columbia* was launched.

After arriving at Stanford, Ellen Ochoa became interested in a field she never thought of before: optics.

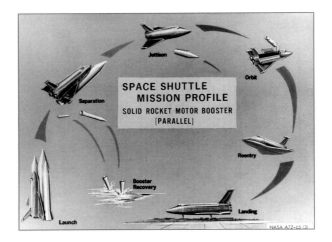

An early diagram showing the use of two parallel solid rocket motor boosters in conjunction with three main engines to launch the proposed space shuttle into orbit.

Optics is a branch of physics. It is the study of light. By looking at the nature of light, new discoveries are made. For example, optical computers use tiny packets of light to process information. Optical computers may be able to process data thousands of times faster than electronic computers.

Ochoa's electrical engineering professor was Joseph Goodman. He was known all over the world for his knowledge of optics. He became Ochoa's graduate advisor. "Ask anyone across the country," Ochoa said, referring to optics, "and there's one person they talk about. That's Joe Goodman."[5]

4

Inventor

Under the guidance of Joseph Goodman, Ellen Ochoa immersed herself in the study of optics. She did a great deal of work with lasers. A laser is a device that makes an intense beam of light. A laser can be used to bore a hole in something as hard as steel or diamond. Or a laser beam can be used for delicate eye surgery or to painlessly drill decayed teeth. Engineers use laser beams to build tunnels. The word *laser* is taken from Light Amplification by Stimulated Emission of Radiation.

Part of optics involves splitting a laser light beam into two beams. This is creating a hologram. Ellen Ochoa worked in this area, creating three-dimensional images. This is useful in designing engine parts and would later be used in the space shuttle equipment.

Ellen Ochoa worked on an optical system to guide robots in space. The system gave the robots the ability to find and identify objects. In 1981, Ochoa received her master's degree in electrical engineering from Stanford University. She continued her optical research as she worked toward her doctorate. During this time, she was winning praise as a classical flutist. She performed a solo with the symphony orchestra at Stanford.

Ellen Ochoa later recalled the moment when space travel became a possibility for her. "Some friends of mine were applying to the astronaut program, so that's when I decided to find out more about the program." She added that the more she learned, she got "real excited about doing it."[1] At the time, another bright young Stanford graduate, Sally Ride, was waiting to be assigned a place on the next space shuttle.

Ellen Ochoa fit the bill for an astronaut very well. NASA was looking for special people skilled in math and science. The agency wanted people who could work well in a team. The ideal astronaut would have other interests as well. NASA wanted well-rounded people who could relax and have fun. They also needed people with either pilot training or an advanced degree. Basic requirements were that applicants have good eyesight, be of average height and weight, and be younger than forty years of age. NASA wanted confident people who could study a problem and solve it calmly.

The application process was long and difficult. It was not easy to get into the astronaut program. But now Ellen Ochoa was seriously considering it. First she would get her doctorate from Stanford—NASA was much more favorable to applicants with a doctorate degree.

In 1982, two years after Ellen Ochoa graduated from San Diego State University, her mother graduated, too.

Rosanne Ochoa received her degree *summa cum laude,* or with greatest honors. She had a 3.9 grade point average. She had worked for this day for twenty-two years. She was sixty-two years old.

Rosanne Ochoa's own mother, Ellen's grandmother, had suffered a severe stroke. Rosanne Ochoa, who had spent her life caring for her children, now took on the care of her mother. For three years she was caregiver, until her mother needed more professional care. Now free of family duties, Rosanne Ochoa joined the classified advertising department of *The San Diego Union.* She worked there for the next sixteen years, until she was eighty years old.

Also in 1982, Sally Ride received her assignment. She would launch into space in 1983, the first American woman to fly in space. (The first woman in space had been a Soviet, Valentina V. Tereshkova, who flew on August 16, 1963.)

Ellen Ochoa watched as Sally Ride blasted off aboard the *Challenger* space shuttle on Mission STS-7. Ride was an inspiration to girls and women everywhere. Ellen Ochoa's plans to become an astronaut were strengthened. Ochoa had spent most of her time at Stanford on optical research and she wrote her doctoral dissertation on the subject. (All Ph.D. candidates must write a detailed research paper on what they have worked on, before being awarded a doctorate.)

In 1985, Ellen Ochoa received a doctorate in electrical engineering from Stanford University. She was now a member of the Optical Society of America and the Phi Beta Kappa honor society. Ochoa decided to apply to be an astronaut, but she was not accepted. Every year, about two thousand people applied, but only one hundred were picked for further interviews. Ochoa was not one of the hundred in 1985.

Ellen Ochoa did not waste any time feeling disappointed when she was not accepted into the astronaut program. She immediately went to work at Sandia National Laboratories in Livermore, California, owned and funded by the United States government. She continued her work in optical research, focusing on systems useful in space. She worked on a system that gave robots sight. This would enable them to be used in repair work outside the space shuttle.

At Sandia National Laboratories, Ochoa worked with other research scientists and was named coinventor of three systems in optics. She earned patents for her inventions. One of her systems inspected objects. One identified objects and could recognize them. The third system made the objects under study clearer.

Patents

A patent is an official government document that gives the inventor the right to use or sell an invention over a set period of time, usually seventeen years. To receive a patent, the invention must be new and useful. Patents are given to encourage new inventions.

Ochoa at work at Sandia National Laboratories. She concentrated on optics research there.

When Ellen Ochoa's older brother, Monte Ochoa, got his pilot's license, Ellen decided to follow him into the sky. She signed up for flying lessons. "I wanted to be an astronaut," she said, "and I thought I should learn more about aviation."[2]

Ochoa continued working at Sandia National Laboratories and applying to be an astronaut. Meanwhile, space shuttle launches had become routine. Then on January 28, 1986, another space shuttle was launched from Kennedy Space Center. A female astronaut was aboard: Judith Resnik. But this mission was special because of the presence of another woman, teacher Christa McAuliffe. She was to be a teacher from space, with her lessons going from outer space into the classrooms of the world. She went through a long process at NASA before being selected for the Teacher-in-Space program. It was hoped McAuliffe's lessons would stimulate interest in space among the students who saw them.

The *Challenger* space shuttle on which McAuliffe and the others were riding had been in space nine times before. On the morning of the launch, the skies were clear and blue. Hundreds had gathered at Kennedy Space Center to watch the liftoff. Millions of people across the country, including schoolchildren, watched on television. Billions of people watched from around the world.

Just seventy-three seconds after liftoff, the *Challenger* exploded. Excitement and joy turned to shock and sorrow. All seven aboard the space shuttle, including McAuliffe, were killed. The space shuttle program had been flying for five years. Everyone knew there were risks, but the tragic disaster shook NASA as nothing had before. People had seen seven bright, courageous, smiling young Americans wave to the world as they boarded the *Challenger,* and in a little more than a minute, they were all dead.

A NASA inquiry later discovered that a faulty O-ring seal had contributed to the accident. O-shaped rings were used to seal joints on the rocket booster. January 28 was a bitter-cold day and icicles hung from the shuttle. The cold weather may have made the O-rings brittle. A flame burst from one of the O-rings. The rocket fuel ignited, triggering the deadly explosion.

Many people in America were so horrified by the *Challenger* disaster that they questioned the future of the

The space shuttle *Challenger* takes flight on June 18, 1983.

space shuttle. Was it worth it to risk lives in this way? Ellen Ochoa grieved with the rest of America over the tragedy. But she did not change her mind about her own plans. She continued to apply to the astronaut program.

Ellen Ochoa now joined NASA's Ames Research Center in Mountain View, California. She worked on the development of a computer system in space. Soon, she was promoted to chief of the intelligent systems technology branch. Ochoa was recognized as an expert in optics and computers. She gave talks at technical conventions. She wrote articles for scientific journals.

The space shuttle program was put on hold after the *Challenger* disaster. New safety measures were put into effect. But NASA continued to accept new astronaut trainees. Ochoa's unique skill in optics and computer hardware finally got somebody's attention. In 1987, NASA chose Ellen Ochoa as one of the one hundred applicants who would be given a closer look. Ochoa continued to work at Mountain View as the application process moved ahead. NASA would whittle the one hundred down to twenty-three. Those twenty-three would officially become astronauts.

As the selection process moved along, Ellen Ochoa was notified that she had been honored with the Hispanic Engineer Albert Baez Award for outstanding technical contribution to humanity and the most prominent engineer in government award. Ochoa had also qualified for her private pilot's license. She waited for word from NASA. In January 1990, the decision came in.

She had been chosen to form the next astronaut team with twenty-two others. She was the first Latina ever chosen for this select group.

Ellen Ochoa said of hearing the news of her selection, "It was so competitive that I was ecstatic to be selected."[3] NASA was back in business after the *Challenger* loss. Space shuttles were flying again. Preparations were beginning for a project NASA had dreamed of for decades. The International Space Station was soon to be a reality.

Before her training as an astronaut began, Ellen Ochoa fell in love with fellow research engineer Coe Fulmer Miles of Molalla, Oregon. They were married and would go to Texas together. Ellen Ochoa was embarking on a more challenging time in her life, now with the support of her husband.

"She's always been very diligent about studying and working for what she wanted to do." She is "calm, rational and thoughtful."[4] Tyler Ochoa, Ellen Ochoa's brother, describes his sister upon learning the news of her selection to become an astronaut.

5

Training to Be an Astronaut

Ellen Ochoa arrived at Lyndon B. Johnson Space Center in late 1990 to begin training. Thirty-three-year-old Ochoa was in excellent physical condition. She hiked, bicycled, and played volleyball. But the training she faced would be physically harder than anything she had ever done before. There would also be mental challenges. She would be going into a strange and dangerous new environment that few people ever experience. She had to be ready for anything.

Ellen Ochoa had earned a doctorate, but her education was only beginning at Johnson Space Center. She had courses in geology, oceanography, meteorology, astronomy, and medicine. In the class on medicine, Ochoa would learn about some of the physical symptoms astronauts feel in space.

When the space shuttle goes into orbit, body fluids move to the head. The face gets puffy. The astronauts feel like they are coming down with a head cold. The curve of the spine straightens. Astronauts might grow a little taller in space. They might also suffer slight backaches. Not all astronauts have really strong symptoms, but some do. Space sickness causes the skin to become pale. Cold sweats, dizziness, and nausea can occur. There is medicine for space sickness, and usually the condition goes away by itself soon after the astronauts settle into orbit. Still, it is important for astronaut trainees to know what to expect.

A main course in Ellen Ochoa's training was space-travel survival. NASA wanted her to be ready in case the spacecraft had to land in an unplanned place on earth. It could be forced to land in the ocean, a jungle, or a desert. She had to learn to use a parachute as part of her survival skills. The astronauts needed to know how to stay alive on the water or in the dangerous wilderness.

Ellen Ochoa was prepared for anything that could happen in space. NASA teachers made sure things broke during training so the astronauts would learn how to fix them. NASA did not want the astronauts to be surprised by systems that went down. They needed to expect this to happen sometimes and to know how to repair the systems. Every astronaut on each mission had to be familiar with everything.

Ellen Ochoa enjoyed learning a lot of new things. "Being an astronaut allows you to learn continuously, like you do in school," she said. She also liked the variety. "One flight you're working on atmospheric research.

Lyndon B. Johnson Space Center

NASA has multiple sites in the United States. Space voyages are launched in the United States from Kennedy Space Center in Florida. But the training and operation center for NASA is at Johnson Space Center. This is where Mission Control guides and tracks the spaceflights. Johnson Space Center is located in east Texas in Houston, near the Gulf of Mexico.

The next, it's bone-density studies," she said.[1] It is important to study bone density during spaceflight because space travelers can experience bone-density loss. NASA designs exercises to prevent this.

NASA used simulators—devices that imitate real situations—to show the astronaut trainees what it is like in space. Ellen Ochoa worked in a large water-filled tank wearing scuba gear. This was similar to the feeling of weightlessness in space. Getting ready for the feeling of weightlessness was a major part of the training.

There is very little gravity in space. This is called microgravity. Everything, including people, just floats. Ellen Ochoa and the other trainees had never felt anything like this. So they had to practice floating until they were able to grab onto objects.

Ochoa could already pilot a small plane, but she had to learn how to pilot a jet plane. With her fellow trainees, she rode in the KC-135 jet aircraft built to get astronauts ready for liftoff. If someone had not experienced the violent sensation of launch, the moment could be very frightening. The KC-135 exercises prepared the trainees to expect the shocking sensation.

The KC-135 soared high in the sky in an arc. When it reached the highest point of the arc, it flew straight down. It was more thrilling than the wildest roller-coaster ride. The KC-135 made thirty to forty steep ascents and descents. It was nicknamed the Vomit Comet because more than one astronaut became very sick during the exercises. The lessons learned on the KC-135 were that launches are very dramatic and you had to keep doing your assigned tasks even if you were sick.

One of the hardest things an astronaut has to learn is to live and work in a space suit. The space suit is a very complex thing. It has twenty thousand parts. It provides the astronaut with oxygen and keeps the astronaut cool in hot temperatures and warm in cold temperatures. The space suit is like a one-person spacecraft in itself. It protects the astronaut and makes it possible to survive in the dangerous environment of space.

Even the simplest movements are difficult when astronauts are wearing a space suit. Just reaching across their chest to turn off a switch must be done in a series of movements. Some astronaut trainees felt like they were trapped in a plastic pipe when they put on the space suit. People wanting to enter the space program are tested for claustrophobia—the fear of being enclosed in tight places. If they have any signs of this, they are rejected by NASA. They could never function

Ellen Ochoa laughs as she's strapped into a aircraft cockpit training device at Vance Air Force Base in Enid, Oklahoma, in July 1990.

in a space suit. Ellen Ochoa experienced no problems with a space suit.

Even the space gloves that go with the suit are very complicated. Ochoa's hands were carefully measured for her pair of gloves. The perfectly fitting gloves must be strong to protect the hands. They must also allow the astronaut to make precise movements. The astronaut must be able to pick up a dime with the gloves on. This is necessary because of the delicate work done in space.

Ellen Ochoa also trained in the space shuttle mission simulator to get used to the feeling of when the rockets ignite and the shuttle takes off. She spent many hours practicing what to do before a flight. She learned about the tasks she would perform in space, especially work with the robotic arm. Ochoa was having many different kinds of experiences getting ready for flight in space. "One day I could fly in a high-performance jet," she said. "Another day I could scuba dive in our big training pool."[2] Clearly, not only was she not discouraged by the rigors of training, she was also having fun.

Ellen Ochoa passed the training course at Johnson Space Center without problems. In July 1991, she officially became an astronaut. She had apparently impressed NASA officials during her training, because she was assigned a place on a mission scheduled for 1993. Ochoa felt very lucky to be assigned a launch so quickly. Many astronauts had waited a number of years before getting a flight. It would be just three years after being selected for the astronaut class that Ochoa would go into space.

Dr. Ellen Ochoa (left), the first Latina astronaut, and Major Eileen M. Collins (right), the first woman to be named as a pilot candidate, begin their first day of candidate training at NASA in Houston, Texas, on July 16, 1990.

Ellen Ochoa climbs into a single-person life raft while floating in a pool at Elgin Air Force Base in Pensacola, Florida, during water-survival exercises.

Ochoa admitted that one of the things that attracted her to the space program was the "wow-factors of blastoff [and] weightlessness." She added, "What engineer wouldn't want those experiences?"[3]

When Rosanne Ochoa heard that her daughter had a launch date, she was proud and excited. All of Ochoa's family and friends shared the excitement of the coming flight. They always thought she would go far with her intelligence and hard work, but nobody quite expected something like this.

Ellen Ochoa took some time away from the Johnson Space Center to return to her hometown of La Mesa in January 1992. It was for a very special occasion. The *Challenger* Center for Space Science Education had been set up in Parkway Junior High where Ochoa had once been a student.

Challenger centers had been established throughout the United States. They were started and funded by the families of the seven who died in the *Challenger* disaster. The families wanted their loved ones to be remembered through a program that benefited the young. The ill-fated *Challenger* flight had been dedicated to education. Christa McAuliffe and the entire crew cared deeply about educating children in science. Young girls, especially, could see that no goal was beyond their reach just because of their gender.

Ellen Ochoa wanted to be present at the dedication of the center at Parkway. The exhibit copied the space center in Houston as much as possible. It had two laboratories, a Mission Control center, and a simulated spacecraft. It was not just something to look at—it was a real hands-on learning experience for the students.

Other *Challenger* centers around the country focused on different aspects of space, such as human landings on the moon and Mars. But the Parkway center studied Halley's Comet, a comet that can be seen by people on earth every seventy-six years.

Ellen Ochoa was overjoyed to see such a wonderful science project at Parkway. Especially exciting for her was seeing the way young girls like Hazel Richards were getting involved. "You don't have to be a perfect science student to be able to do any of this," thirteen-year-old Hazel said as she sat at Mission Control at the *Challenger* Center. "It's wonderful," thirteen-year-old Jennifer Lindsay said. "I've always loved science, and this just blows my mind."[4] When Ellen Ochoa was thirteen years old, in these same classrooms, she could not have imagined such an opportunity. And even if there had been such an opportunity, girls like Hazel and Jennifer would probably not have been in the midst of it.

There was a particularly happy moment for Ellen Ochoa as she watched Jennifer busily working a small robotic arm to move objects. In her upcoming space shuttle mission, Ochoa would be working the real version of the same thing.

In her frequent visits to schools after being chosen as an astronaut, Ellen Ochoa often told the students, "Don't be afraid to reach for the stars. I believe a good education can take you anywhere on earth and beyond."[5] At her middle-school alma mater, Ochoa watched young girls doing just that: reaching for the stars.

A week before Ellen Ochoa would ride into space, Paz Jensen, her former calculus teacher at Grossmont High School, commented on Ochoa's impact on girls and young women. Jensen was now an instructor at San Diego's Cuyamaca College in the eastern part of the county. She said Ellen Ochoa was having a powerful impact on high school and college students.

Ellen Ochoa was about to become the first Latina in space. It was six years since the *Challenger* tragedy, and the possibility of accidents was always present. Ochoa was not afraid, but she was realistic. She said, "I think if you are not a little scared, you don't understand the risks."[6] Ochoa understood the mission she was about to undertake. She understood it inside and out. So she was a little bit scared. But that would not stop her from the adventure of her life.

"She's become a role model to my students. Here's someone who grew up in the neighborhood, who is an inspiration to everyone to keep on going."[7] Paz Jensen on Ellen Ochoa.

The First Flight

Space shuttles are space transportation systems or STSs. The number after STS indicates how many flights have been made. The first space shuttle mission was STS-1. Ellen Ochoa was scheduled to ride STS-56, the fifty-sixth shuttle mission.

There have been just six space shuttles made: *Columbia, Challenger, Discovery, Atlantis, Enterprise,* and *Endeavour. Endeavour* was used on the ground for training until 1992. As Ochoa prepared for her flight, just four operating shuttles remained, *Challenger* having been lost in 1986. Ellen Ochoa would be aboard *Discovery.*

Ellen Ochoa said of her upcoming journey, "There's nothing else I'd rather be doing," but she admitted that when the moment of takeoff came she would be thinking "about a lot of different things."[1] She added that she had been well prepared for this flight. She would know how to deal with whatever came up. Every effort had been made to make STS-56 a safe journey.

When April 6, 1993, dawned, the weather was perfect. All systems were ready to go. Ellen Ochoa walked with her crewmates toward the launchpad. She was a mission specialist. Kenneth Cameron was flight commander. Stephen S. Oswald was the pilot. Kenneth D. Cockrell and Michael Foale were, like Ochoa, mission specialists.

Ochoa explained, "One of my primary jobs on the shuttle is to handle the science experiments and to make sure that they were operating correctly."[2]

Ellen Ochoa described her feelings at the moment of takeoff. The first time an astronaut is launched is a dramatic experience. Ochoa was thrilled by the thunder of the engines. She felt the power of acceleration against gravity as the shuttle leaped into the sky. "There was a lot of light and a lot of rumbling and vibration," Ochoa said. Most of it happened in the first minute and a half. Then "the ride got a lot smoother."[3] Ochoa heard the main engines shut down as the space shuttle entered orbit.

A German space agency group had worked with NASA to develop a space lab system. This system allowed computer commands to be made to the experiments. The experiments could reply. Even experiments outside the space shuttle could obey commands and answer. This system was on board STS-56.

The nine-day mission included atmospheric tests and a study of the sun. NASA wanted to know the effect of solar activity on the earth's atmosphere. NASA hoped to

On its second attempt, the space shuttle *Discovery* lifts off from the launch pad on April 8, 1993. The first attempt at launch was halted at T-11 seconds on April 6.

learn more about what was causing the loss of ozone in the earth's atmosphere.

Given the importance of preserving the ozone layer, scientists want to find out if the ozone layer is being damaged by manufactured products like plastics. Do pollutants from these products rise into the atmosphere and make holes in the ozone layer? Do they cause the ozone layer to grow thinner and less effective against harmful rays from the sun? NASA was attempting to find out in this mission whether natural events like volcanic eruptions might be damaging the ozone layer. NASA wanted to study how much pollution was in the upper atmosphere and what was causing it.

Ozone Layer

Above the earth is a layer of gases called the ozone layer. Ozone is a bluish form of oxygen that blocks solar radiation. In the ozone layer there is atomic oxygen, ordinary oxygen, and ozone. The ozone layer is found about ten to twenty miles (sixteen to thirty-two kilometers) above the surface of the earth. Ozone absorbs and protects earth from the most harmful rays of the sun. This protective blanket is very important to the earth and its people.

Ellen Ochoa explained, "If we had that ultraviolet radiation [from the sun] reaching the surface of the earth, it would cause a lot of problems in humans like skin cancer as well as sunburn . . . and it may have a very big impact on other plant and animal life."[4]

Since the 1980s, scientists have noted lower levels of ozone over Antarctica during the winter. The growing ozone hole was frightening. More heat from the sun breaking through appeared to cause the ice in Antarctica to melt faster.

Scientists fear that the ozone hole seen over Antarctica may appear over the Arctic regions, too. NASA scientist Azadeh Tabazadeh noted that 700 million people live in the Arctic area, including parts of Alaska, Canada, Scandinavia, and Russia. A damaged ozone layer could cause crops to fail. People in the affected areas could starve.

This space shuttle mission was not just gathering interesting facts about the atmosphere. It was a serious attempt to find out what was damaging a vital part of our atmosphere—our ozone layer.

Ellen Ochoa and her crewmates used a $55 million laboratory aboard the shuttle to do their tests. It was called Atmospheric Laboratory for Applications and Science (ATLAS). It gathered and stored information. Later, scientists would study the data gathered.

Early in the mission, the space shuttle had a problem. One of the atmospheric collecting computers crashed. With some help from ground controllers, Ellen Ochoa had the system running again in forty-four minutes.

During the mission, space shuttle commander Kenneth Cameron used his ham radio to talk to Russia's *Mir* space station. It was a historic moment. It was the first ship-to-ship conversation between a shuttle and

This photo of the Strait of Gibraltar was taken aboard the *Discovery* on April 17, 1993. A small bank of clouds marks the passage between Spain and Morocco at the western edge of the Mediterranean Sea. The cities of Cadiz on the Atlantic coast of Spain and Malaga on the Mediterranean coast, as well as Tangier, Morocco (facing the strait), can be seen.

another spacecraft. Two people held the brief conversation as the space shuttle passed the Russian space station over South America.

An exciting part of the mission for Ellen Ochoa was connecting by radio to a group of students at Parkway Middle School in La Mesa where she had been a student. Ochoa carried into space with her a Parkway Patriots patch from the school uniform. She also carried with her a photograph of one hundred civic leaders and ordinary citizens of La Mesa posing to replicate a 1920s photograph. The photo was taken to celebrate the eightieth anniversary of the founding of La Mesa. The photograph would be returned to La Mesa when the space shuttle landed. Having been in space, it would be a treasured part of La Mesa history.

On the space mission, Ellen Ochoa skillfully used the robotic arm to send the satellite *Spartan* toward the sun. Then she brought it back safely. The *Spartan* collected

MIR

The Soviet Union launched several manned space stations called the Salyut program between 1971 and 1982. On February 20, 1986, a new space station was launched. Called *Mir*, meaning both "peace" and "the world," this space station was larger and had six docking ports. More modules could be added to it. Other spacecraft could dock and visit the crew inside *Mir*. NASA planned to dock with *Mir* in 1995.

extremely valuable data. The success of this part of the mission was vital.

From orbit, Ochoa radioed Mission Control and described the view: "It's really a pretty sight to be in this altitude with the sun streaming in through the windows. The most exciting thing was looking at earth from up there. It was beautiful."[5]

The *Discovery* space shuttle returned to earth on April 17, 1993, at 7:37 A.M., in a perfect landing. Ellen Ochoa and her crewmates had physical examinations and discussed the mission with NASA officials. Then, as soon as she could, Ochoa went back to her hometown of La Mesa. She had connected with the Parkway students by radio from orbit. Now she wanted to share her adventure with them in person.

In the same room where the Parkway Junior High students had spoken to Ochoa in space, they would now see her face-to-face. "It was totally different meeting her," said eighth-grader Jason Wood. "I thought she would be a big celebrity, but she's just a normal person." Jason noted that Ochoa went to school right in La Mesa, and maybe someday he would go into space like her.[6]

Veronica Aldrete had spent the last month making a scrapbook about Ellen Ochoa. Now Ellen Ochoa's autograph was in that scrapbook. "I felt honored to meet her," Veronica said. "She's an admirable person."[7]

When Ochoa first started talking to the students, she felt shy. But as she talked about her mission, she became more comfortable. She showed the students pictures of

Crewmembers pose for an onboard (inflight) portrait on the aft flight deck of the *Discovery*. In front are Commander Kenneth Cameron (left) and Mission Specialist I (MSI) Michael Foale; in back are (left to right) MS3 Ellen Ochoa, pilot Stephen S. Oswald, and MS2 Kenneth D. Cockrell. The crew is positioned next to the on-orbit station with the earth's blue and white surface appearing in overhead windows above them.

This *Discovery* mission patch is a pictorial representation of the STS-56 Atmospheric Laboratory for Applications and Science 2 (ATLAS-2) mission as seen from the crew's viewpoint. Surnames of the commander and pilot are inscribed in the earth field, with the surnames of the mission specialists appearing in the space background.

Australia, the northern lights, and the Himalaya mountains taken from space. She also had photos of herself using the robotic arm.

Ochoa gave the students the Parkway Patriots patch that had gone into space with her. She also gave them framed pictures of the crew of STS-56. The students gave Ochoa a school polo shirt and a baseball cap. It had been a wonderful homecoming for Ellen Ochoa.

Ochoa left Parkway and hurried away to her other childhood school, Northmont Elementary. After another warm reception, Ochoa said, "I hope some students got encouragement" to travel into space.[8]

Ochoa did not just share her adventures with students at her the schools she had attended. She visited Belvedere Junior High School, Cantwell Elementary, and the Salesian Boys and Girls Club. Still very excited about her space journey, Ochoa wore her navy-blue jumpsuit with the colorful NASA patches.

Ellen Ochoa immediately bonded with her young audiences by talking about food. Discussing the astronauts' favorites, she said, "One of our favorite foods is tortillas. They taste good. They're flat and pack well. Bread creates crumbs that, when you're in space, just fly around."[9]

Ochoa then discussed the serious goals of the mission. She told the students that NASA needed to find out what was damaging the ozone layer that protected earth.

At one school, eleven-year-old Ivan Aviles was very impressed. "It's the first time I've ever seen an astronaut and I think she has a nice attitude. I wouldn't mind being an astronaut myself."[10] At Smyth Elementary School in San Diego, Ellen Ochoa was hailed as "an authentic hero" by Councilman Juan Carlos Vargas.[11] Nine-year-old Brenda Dominguez said, "I never thought a person like her would come here to see us."[12] The students commented on Ochoa's bravery. Most of all they were amazed to actually see someone in the flesh who had done something as amazing as fly into space.

At a May 1993 assembly that included students from Granger Junior High, Gompers Secondary School, Memorial Academy, National City Middle School, and Ochoa's Grossmont High School, the gathered students delighted Ochoa by singing "Happy Birthday" to her. She had just celebrated her thirty-fifth birthday. Ochoa amused them by talking about the times the space crew did silly things like play with water bubbles in space. Alejandra Quevedo summed it all up by saying, "She's wonderful."[13]

In 1993, Ellen Ochoa received the Congressional Hispanic Caucus Medallion of Excellence Role Model Award for her achievements in space. Ochoa always stressed that although she is proud of her Latino heritage, ethnic background is of less importance than "motivation, perseverance, and desire—the desire to participate in a voyage of discovery."[14]

There are about two thousand career Latino employees at NASA. They serve in many jobs, including electronics and aeronautical and space engineering. There are Latino inventors, test pilots, physicists, and trainers.

Ellen Ochoa was the first Latina woman to enter space, but she was preceded by two Latino men. Franklin Chang-Diaz, originally from Costa Rica, became the first Latino to ride a space shuttle on a mission in 1986. Lieutenant Colonel Sidney Gutierrez was the second Latino. With ancestors from Spain and Mexico, Gutierrez was from Albuquerque, New Mexico.

Ellen Ochoa hoped to inspire more young people like eleven-year-old Sergio Moreno from San Ysidro, California. After hearing Ochoa speak, he said, "I learned that if she can do it, any person can do it." His little sister added, "You, me, and everybody."[15]

"They often don't see people with Hispanic last names doing something like flying in space. It's something they might dream about. Just having that extra bit of encouragement can get them started."[16] Ellen Ochoa talks about speaking to students in Logan Heights, California, a multiracial community, after her 1993 space flight.

Payload Commander

No longer a rookie astronaut, Ellen Ochoa was payload commander on her second flight into space. A mission specialist as well, she was now also in charge of all the scientific studies on board. Ochoa would make sure the atmospheric data was being properly collected.

STS-66 on the *Atlantis* space shuttle would continue the work done on Ochoa's first mission into space. The crew would gather data about the condition of the ozone layer over the earth. They wanted exact information about the harmful gases that man was sending into the atmosphere. They also wanted to see what part the radiation from the sun played in the ozone layer.

There were many experiments on board, including one testing the effect of weightlessness on rats. There were ten pregnant rats on the space shuttle. They would be the first pregnant mammals to fly on a space shuttle.

Ellen Ochoa would also operate the robotic arm as she had done on her first flight. This time she would recover the satellite after it had completed its mission.

The orbiter *Atlantis* launches with a nearly on-time liftoff into clear
Florida skies on November 3, 1994.

The mission was scheduled from November 3 to November 14, 1994. It was the seventh and last shuttle mission of the year. It was the sixty-sixth time a space shuttle had flown. NASA had remodeled the *Atlantis* with new wiring and other equipment. It would dock on a later mission with the Russian *Mir* space station. The planned docking of the space shuttle and *Mir* reflected improved relations between the United States and Russia.

Aboard the *Atlantis* was Jean-Francois Clervoy from France. He represented the European nations. Another European, Ulf Merbold, was on the *Mir* space station at the same time. The journey into space was becoming an international project.

Very complex instruments were aboard *Atlantis.* The Atmospheric Laboratory for Application and Science

USSR Becomes Russia

In 1987, Mikhail Gorbachev began economic and political reforms in Communist Russia. This led to the breakup of the Soviet Union under Communism. In December 1991, the Communist flag, the hammer and sickle, was taken down. The Russian flag, bearing a white stripe on top, a blue stripe in the middle, and a red stripe at the bottom, was raised. The Communist Party, which had dominated Russia since 1917, lost power. This was followed by an end to the Cold War rivalry between the United States and the Soviet Union.

(ATLAS) was joined by a new satellite to be launched and then recovered by the robotic arm: *CRISTA-SPAS*.

CRISTA-SPAS, which stands for Cryogenic Infrared Spectrometers and Telescopes for the Atmosphere–Shuttle Pallet Satellite, was a satellite designed and made at the University of Wuppertal in Germany. It had three telescopes to see earth clearly. It made global maps of temperature and trace gases. The $35 million *CRISTA-SPAS* was a joint experiment between the United States and Germany. Students at the University of Wuppertal and two of their professors had a major role in developing the satellite. They did the calculations, designed the optics, and organized the project. After the mission, German students would process the data. The *CRISTA-SPAS* was to be sent from the cargo bay of the space shuttle, where it could fly free. Away from the pollution of the shuttle, it could perform very accurate tests of gases in the atmosphere.

The timing of this space shuttle mission was very important. Scientists had noted that the loss of ozone over Antarctica begins late in August. Starting in October, the ozone builds up again. Ellen Ochoa noted, "We'll have the opportunity to try to understand more about how the atmosphere recovers from this annual event."[1]

Although most scientists believe that man-made chemicals sent into the atmosphere harm the ozone layer, exactly what happens is not known. *CRISTA-SPAS* was designed to discover how and why the ozone decreases and then builds up again.

Ellen Ochoa, payload commander, is seen here on the *Atlantis*'s forward flight deck having just completed an operation with the Remote Manipulator System (RMS) arm.

The liftoff of *Atlantis* in November was not without problems. The weather at Kennedy Space Center was fine, but that was not all that mattered. NASA wanted to be sure that if the shuttle needed to land unexpectedly at another site after liftoff, the weather there would also be acceptable. Spain and Morocco were two emergency landing sites. The weather in Spain was bad and there were worrisome winds in Morocco. But eventually the winds calmed in Morocco and the launch was approved.

When the shuttle was in orbit, Ellen Ochoa inspected the fifty-foot-long robotic arm that would be used to launch and recover *CRISTA-SPAS*. Ochoa had described the robotic arm as "a lot like your own arm. It has a wrist joint. It has an elbow joint and it has a shoulder joint." She said it operated like a video game.[2]

The *Atlantis* crew was divided into two teams, the Red and the Blue, each with three members. The teams did twelve-hour shifts so there would always be a crew working. Ellen Ochoa was on the Red Team along with mission commander Donald R. McMonagle and mission specialist Joseph Tanner. French astronaut Clervoy was on the Blue Team. On Friday, November 4, at 7:30 A.M., Clervoy launched the satellite *CRISTA-SPAS* from the shuttle using the robotic arm. The release took place 164 nautical miles above Germany.

For eight days, the astronauts used *CRISTA-SPAS* to study the sun and the atmosphere. It would measure what humans had put into the air and what role the sun played in the ozone layer. Even small changes in the sun's radiation can make a huge difference on earth. A one percent change in solar radiation (sunlight) can cause a drought or a cold period on earth.

Ellen Ochoa took a short break from her shuttle duties to answer questions posed by honor students at a Washington, D.C., high school. The interview from space was broadcast on WRC-TV.

On Saturday, November 5, Ellen Ochoa and her crewmates got dramatic views of an Atlantic hurricane forming. They sent the pictures of a swirling Hurricane Florence to earth. The photos appeared on the television weather channel.

A Tribute to Stacey

Stacey Lynn Balascio grew up with Ellen Ochoa in La Mesa, California. Both graduated from Grossmont High School and both were good students. Balascio was a Reserve Officers Training Corps (ROTC) cadet and an engineering student with a bright future. Four days before her college graduation, she was killed in an auto accident. Ochoa took Balascio's class ring with her on the 1994 *Atlantis* flight. When Ochoa returned, she presented the ring to Balascio's parents. "It was my tribute to her," Ochoa said.[3]

The *CRISTA-SPAS* satellite was moving about forty-two miles behind the space shuttle. This mission was called the most complete global health check of the atmosphere that was ever done.

On Sunday Ochoa and the other two members of the Red Team exercised on their bicycles. In space it is vitally important for astronauts to maintain their physical fitness. The harsh extraterrestrial environment can lead to such health problems as bone and muscle loss.

CRISTA-SPAS was showing low ozone levels over Antarctica, which was expected. Evidence of high levels of chemicals introduced by man was found. One free atom of chlorine, a nonmetallic element used to make dyes and other products, can destroy thousands of ozone molecules.[4]

The astronauts observed ozone-rich air mixing with Antarctic air. The ozone layer was beginning to improve.

This was the beginning of the annual cycle of the ozone layer sealing the hole with the onset of winter.

On Tuesday, November 8, Ellen Ochoa and her crewmates discussed the progress of the mission during an in-flight press conference. Mission Commander McMonagle reported that all the astronauts had voted in the national elections before the flight. He also described great success with the atmospheric measuring devices.

Ochoa's Red Team worked to maneuver the shuttle for a better view of the sun. They also began to prepare for the recovery of *CRISTA-SPAS* on Saturday. They were getting a little closer to the satellite. Ellen Ochoa reported seeing as many as thirteen or fourteen layers of gases in the atmosphere during sunsets. The crew took photographs of the sunsets with a telephoto lens.[5]

Ochoa noted that the Atmospheric Trace Molecule Spectroscopy (ATMOS) could measure as many as thirty to forty trace gases at once. It could find extremely small traces—even a few parts in a billion. "Even though the quantities are small," Ochoa said, "these gases can play a large part in ozone destruction."[6]

On November 10, the mission had lasted longer than ten days, so the astronauts got a few hours off. Ochoa used what free time she had to play the flute for fun and relaxation.

On November 11, some results of the atmospheric tests were in. The astronauts had learned important information. Refrigerators had been using chemicals

Masses of clouds over the Atlantic Ocean serve as the backdrop for this close-up scene of the Cryogenic Infrared Spectrometers and Telescopes for the Atmosphere (CRISTA). The crew deployed the CRISTA-SPAS on November 4, 1994, and the tandem remained in free-flight until November 12, 1994, when it was retrieved by the RMS controlled by payload commander Ellen Ochoa.

considered very harmful to the atmosphere. Then manufacturers converted to using freon-2. The new data confirmed that freon-2 was doing less harm to the atmosphere than the previous chemical. It was hoped that even safer refrigeration methods could be found.

On Saturday, November 12, at 5:00 A.M., Ellen Ochoa prepared to recover *CRISTA-SPAS*. The satellite had been out in space for eight days and its mission was completed. During the maneuver to recover the satellite, Commander McMonagle said the 7,500-pound triangular satellite looked "like a diamond in the sky."[7] *CRISTA-SPAS* was directly above the shuttle. By approaching it from below, the shuttle was using the earth's gravity as a natural brake. This was a rehearsal for the mission in which the space shuttle would dock with *Mir*. It reduced the need to fire jets, which might damage *Mir*.

Ellen Ochoa swung into action with the robotic arm and pulled *CRISTA-SPAS* in. The recovery of the satellite was the high point of the mission. "It was very exciting," Ochoa said, "especially the view of the satellite."[8] The capture of *CRISTA-SPAS* took place just north of Antarctica and south of New Zealand.

"Super! Super!" shouted excited German scientists from the control room at Kennedy Space Center. The Germans celebrated with coffee and gummy bears.[9] Mission Control in Houston told Ochoa and the other astronauts that it was a superb rendezvous. They said, "You've given us some important data and a lot of confidence. Well done."[10]

On November 12, with *CRISTA-SPAS* safely tucked away in the shuttle's cargo bay, Ellen Ochoa ordered the robotic arm to view an icicle that had formed on the door of the cargo bay after a water dump. Television cameras showed the door and latches free of ice. But a big icicle hung on the door. The crew discussed what to do about it. They did not want to damage anything on the outside of the shuttle. They decided to use the robotic arm to knock the icicle off and send it into space. But then the camera on the end of the robotic arm failed. There would be no way of observing the maneuver. The crew decided that the icicle was not a safety risk, so they just left it alone.

One of the scientists looking at the data collected, Mike Gunson, said the *Atlantis* mission provided "a really interesting story to tell about the ozone hole." He added, "I'm really happy with the way things have gone. Enormously successful is almost an understatement at this point."[11]

Atlantis STS-66 prepared to land. The only problems left were weather conditions. The shuttle was scheduled to land at Kennedy Space Center, but the weather had taken a turn for the worse. Tropical Storm Gordon was whipping up high winds and torrents of rain in Florida. The sky was thick with clouds. A landing there was impossible. The landing was moved to Edwards Air Force Base in California's Mojave Desert. Because of the nuisance and expense of bringing the space shuttle from California back to Florida after an Edwards landing, it

A space photograph of Hurricane Florence at its peak over the open waters of the North Atlantic Ocean.

was a last resort, but the safety of the astronauts came first. So on November 14, 1994, at 10:33 A.M., *Atlantis* landed at Edwards.

Ellen Ochoa had completed her second mission in space, performing with her usual skill. She received a flight medal in 1994.

All the data from STS-66 was deposited in the Earth Observing Systems Data Information System Archive at NASA's Goddard Space Flight Center. NASA program scientist Jack Kaye said, "It will be made available to atmospheric scientists around the world."[12]

In 1995, Ellen Ochoa returned to San Diego State University, where she was named 1995 Alumni of the Year. She attended, along with other successful graduates, a gala at the San Diego Convention Center. Her achievements in optics and space were celebrated.

After her 1994 space flight, Ellen Ochoa worked with NASA on the ground. She was a member of the Mission Control team planning the future of America's space program. She worked at Mission Control from 1994 to 1999. Ochoa had thoroughly enjoyed her two missions in space and she wanted to explore space again. At thirty-six and with so much successful experience behind her, she believed she would fly again. It would only be a matter of time before she blasted off once more.

International Space Station

During the years that Ellen Ochoa prepared for and took part in space flights, she also became a mother. Her first son was Wilson, followed by a second son, Jordan. During her first space flight, Wilson was just a baby. Ochoa was gone for several weeks but her son was too young to notice. The next time she was gone for an extended period, Ochoa prepared. She made a tape of herself and her son playing before she left. When Wilson became lonely for his mother, his father played the tape. It made Wilson feel better.

Like many working mothers, Ellen Ochoa found ways to cope with being a career woman and a mother. When she was leaving for a mission and was going to be gone for a period of time, she made a paper chain with a link for each day she would be gone. Ochoa's boys could remove a link each day and see their mother's return growing closer.

Ellen Ochoa's sons enjoyed watching their mother in space. When segments of the space flights were filmed and appeared on television, they eagerly watched. Ochoa tried to do some silly things when she was on camera to entertain her boys. Once she suspended Goldfish crackers in front of her mouth. As they floated in the weightless spacecraft, she opened her mouth and gobbled them up.[1]

"This career takes a lot of time," Ochoa said. "You often have strange hours." Because an astronaut does not have a set schedule, Ochoa admitted, "Child care is an issue. A lot of astronaut women face that."[2]

Ellen Ochoa's husband, Coe Fulmer Miles, is also a research scientist. During her space mission, Ochoa e-mailed her husband every day. When a space mission lasted longer than ten days, Ochoa and her husband had video conferences where they could see each other as they talked.

In 1999, Ellen Ochoa was again given a mission in space. The space shuttle *Discovery* STS-96 mission would be part of a larger effort to assemble the International Space Station (ISS). This was the most complex project ever attempted in space. When complete, the ISS is expected to be four times the size of *Mir*. It will weigh more than 1 million pounds (453,592 kilograms). It will be the size of a 747 jumbo jet on the inside. On the outside, it will be larger than a football field. Led by the United States, the ISS is using the scientific and technical experts and resources of sixteen nations. Taking part are Canada, Japan, Russia, Brazil, and all the members of the European Space Agency.

The ISS was placed in orbit about 250 miles above the earth in 1998. The first large pieces were the Russian control module *Zarya* and the American-made *Unity* node. These two pieces were attached during the December 1998 *Endeavor* STS-88 mission.

Now Ellen Ochoa and her six fellow crew members would prepare the International Space Station for the arrival of the first station crew. Their mission was to dock with the ISS and deliver supplies, which would be used when the first three-person crew arrived to live at the ISS. In October 2000 the crew would arrive for a four-month stay on the ISS.

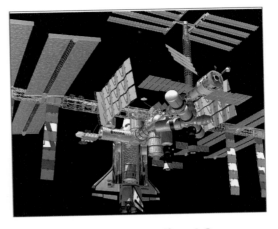

Phase II of the International Space Station (ISS) concept is illustrated here with the space shuttle docked to it. The station is shown here in its completed and fully operational state with elements from the United States, Europe, Canada, Japan, and Russia.

Ochoa and the others on STS-96 delivered almost two tons of supplies, including clothing, computers, and medical equipment. Kent V. Rominger commanded STS-96. The pilot was Rick D. Husband, and there were five mission specialists, including Ochoa and Valery I. Tokarev from the Russian Space Agency.

Ellen Ochoa's specific job was to oversee the transfer of the supplies from the space shuttle to the ISS. The robotic arm would be used to accomplish this. It would be the third time Ochoa would be using the robotic arm in a space mission.

Ochoa first plotted the rendezvous on a laptop computer to make sure the shuttle was going in the right direction. The shuttle approached the ISS from below the space station. Then they did a fly around. After that they came in above the ISS, putting the space station between earth and the shuttle. Ochoa had to work

Astronauts Ellen Ochoa, Joan Higginbotham, and Yvonne Cagle share the podium while attending a forum about women in space. They were included in a panel discussing "Past, Present and Future of Space." Former astronaut Sally Ride is at right.

harder operating the robotic arm this time because she could not directly watch the robotic arm she was guiding. She maneuvered the arm using cameras to see what she was doing.

The docking of the space shuttle and the ISS was very successful. The shuttle crew began loading space suits, cameras, and electronic equipment into the ISS. Two cranes were also loaded for future use in assembling other pieces of the ISS. One of the cranes was made in Russia, the other in the United States. Bags of tools were offloaded from the shuttle to the ISS for future projects.

Ellen Ochoa was not finished using the robotic arm. She also used it for the eight-hour space walk two of the astronauts took. Tammy Jernigan and Dan Barry went outside the space shuttle while Ochoa operated the robotic arm they were riding.

Jernigan rode on the end of the robotic arm as Ochoa maneuvered her into position. This left Jernigan's hands free to use her equipment. She assembled parts of the ISS to make future additions easier. Tammy Jernigan and Dan Barry installed foot restraints and handrails to be used by future astronauts in the construction of the ISS. They also inspected the communications system.

Ellen Ochoa had been working for two years preparing for this mission. She admitted she felt "a very personal attachment to the station."[3] Ochoa believed the ISS had three very vital benefits to humanity. First, it would provide a laboratory for medical advances. Scientists would be able to live on the space station for extended periods, giving them time to observe their experiments. Second, new materials of use to mankind could be manufactured in the weightless space. Third, it was a wonderful chance for international cooperation. "It's just an incredible international venture where you have people from all over the world getting together assembling an incredibly complex vehicle," she said. Ochoa praised all those involved for "working together for items that really benefit people around the world."[4]

Yet another benefit of the ISS is that it provides a wonderful observation station to view earth. Eighty-five percent of planet earth is observable from the ISS, including 95 percent of the world's populations. Storm activity, erosion, and climate changes can be seen and mapped. It will be a twenty-four-hour constant eye in the sky.

When all the supplies were aboard the space station, Ellen Ochoa commented, "We spent a lot of time on this mission stowing supplies, so it should be pretty comfortable."[5]

Discovery spent six days linked to the ISS and met all its goals. But working at the ISS was not all that the mission accomplished. *Discovery* launched another satellite from its cargo bay called *Starshine*. This satellite was a beautiful example of starting international cooperation among the young.

The *Starshine* satellite launched from *Discovery* weighing 86.6 pounds. It was a hollow aluminum ball the size

STS-96 Mission Specialist Ellen Ochoa chats with white room closeout crew members while being checked out for entry into the orbiter *Discovery* **on May 27, 1999.**

of a beach ball. It was covered with 878 polished mirrors, each one inch in diameter. The mirrors were made in Utah to be attached to *Starshine*. But they were polished by students from around the world. The mirrors were shipped to schools in Argentina, Australia, Austria, Belgium, Canada, China, Denmark, England, Finland, Japan, Mexico, New Zealand, Pakistan, South Africa, Spain, Turkey, the United States, and Zimbabwe. All of these young people played a part in launching their own little star. It was sent into orbit 220 miles above the earth.

Teams of elementary-, middle-, and high-school students around the world were assigned the job of tracking the satellite with the use of computers and astronomical equipment. This was a lesson in measuring daily changes in the time it took *Starshine* to circle the earth.

Project Starshine made plans to launch such a satellite every year until 2009. It is a great teaching tool for students to work with real space hardware. It is also a lesson in international cooperation.

Discovery STS-96 landed on June 6, 1999, at Kennedy Space Center in Florida. Every NASA mission has a mission patch. The patch for STS-96 showed the space shuttle circling the earth. It showed the International Space Station and rays of light rising to a star. These images symbolized research and international cooperation.

When Ellen Ochoa was not on a space mission or preparing for one, she was helping others prepare for missions and guiding them from Mission Control in Houston. On October 11, 2000, NASA launched STS-97. The *Endeavour* space shuttle was going into space to build more of the framework for the International Space Station. The mission this time included a Japanese astronaut: Koichi Wakata. He would help further prepare the ISS for the arrival of the crew later in the year. Ellen Ochoa had worked with the robotic arm before. Now she was helping Wakata, who would be operating the arm.

Ellen Ochoa watched the launch of STS-97, and then she and others in Mission Control observed Koichi Wakata dealing with a two-and-a-half hour delay in his robotic arm maneuver. There was a short in the space shuttle's wiring. Wakata was scheduled to operate a fifty-foot-long robotic arm. He would attach a truss to the docking port on the far side of the space station module. (A truss is a support frame. It had to be attached so more pieces of the space station could be added as needed.) As was the case when Ochoa used the robotic arm, Wakata did not have direct sight of his work. He had to use the space vision system. Like Ochoa, he used a laptop computer. Ochoa knew from her own experience how hard this was.

Ellen Ochoa holds her son, Wilson Miles-Ochoa, as she leaves the bus at the Cape Canaveral Air Station Skid Strip on June 7, 1999.

"Mommy, can boys be astronauts, too?"–A question posed by Wilson, Ellen Ochoa's eldest son, one day as they drove past the Johnson Space Center.[7]

When the wiring problem in the space shuttle was resolved, Wakata went to work. When he finally succeeded in putting the truss in place, Ellen Ochoa radioed him, "Koichi, you the man!"[6]

After all the hard work done by many space missions, including STS-96, it was time to celebrate a great moment. A permanent crew would soon arrive at the ISS. After all the missions piecing together modules and adding supports, it was finally happening. All those supplies Ochoa and her crewmates loaded into the ISS would now be used.

On October 31, 2000, *Soyuz* TM-204, a Russian spacecraft, delivered American astronaut Bill Shepherd and Russian cosmonauts Yuri Gidzenko and Sergei Krikalev to the International Space Station to settle in for a long stay. It was like a small apartment, and the men would live there for four months. The ISS would from now on always be staffed with astronauts. Ellen Ochoa and her fellow NASA astronauts were delighted to know that the next time they took a space mission to the ISS, there would be human beings to greet them.

The mission insignia for the STS-96 space flight, the second space shuttle mission dedicated to the assembly of the International Space Station (ISS). The space shuttle *Discovery* is depicted as it is about to carry out the first docking with the new station.

Only a dozen years earlier, engineer Ellen Ochoa learned that there might be a place for her in the space program. Before that she thought being a woman would make such a career unlikely. Now, she was a veteran of three space missions, and she was eager for the next mission.

Not only has Ellen Ochoa been an inspiration to many children and teenagers, but she also helped an older woman achieve her own dream. Rosamond Weinberg from Wombourne, England, had struggled with a learning disability in her youth. She had dyslexia.

(Readers with dyslexia reverse letters. For example, they read the word *was* as *saw,* or they see the letters as being upside down.)

After attending a lecture called "Women Who Dared," which featured Ellen Ochoa among other speakers, Weinberg was so fired up by Ochoa's passionate call for people to follow their dreams that she enrolled in college. At the age of sixty-nine she graduated from California State University at San Marcos. She earned a bachelor's degree in women's studies. She planned to use it to "help women in some way."[8]

As 2002 approached, Ellen Ochoa got another launch date. She would be going into space again to meet the astronauts living on the International Space Station she had helped to build.

Medical Research on the ISS

Medical research on the International Space Station holds great promise. Living cells can be grown in a laboratory aboard the station. Gravity will not be able to interfere with the results. Tissue cultures can be used to find new treatments for cancer. Viruses had been studied on the space shuttle, but the flights were too short for much success. Now, with the space station in permanent orbit, there was time for extended research. New drugs for viruses could be found. Many scientists hope cures may be found for cancer, diabetes, emphysema, and other diseases.

9

Fourth Space Flight and Beyond

Ellen Ochoa prepared for her fourth space flight, which would be aboard the space shuttle *Atlantis*. The STS-110 ten-day mission was another step in the construction of the International Space Station. Carried in the cargo bay was a $600 million truss. The truss was to be the center part of a 300-foot-long support structure. It would be attached to the *Destiny* laboratory module. Made of steel and aluminum by Boeing, it contained 475,000 parts. Filled with wiring, pipes, and computers, the truss would be the backbone of the ISS.

There was something different about this space mission because of what happened seven months earlier in the United States. Because of the terrorist attacks on New York and Washington, D.C., on September 11, 2001, there was great security in place. This would be the first time in NASA's twenty-one-year history that the exact launch time would be kept secret. Instead, NASA said the launch would be sometime between 2:00 P.M. and 6:00 P.M. The arrival of the crew from Houston to Kennedy Space Center was also kept secret. It was announced that they were present only after they landed. "NASA feels you have to do something about security," spokesperson Lisa Malone explained.[1]

There were clear skies over the Atlantic Ocean as the space shuttle prepared for liftoff, but a stiff wind was blowing. A computer problem caused a short delay. But what was on everybody's mind was security. All airplanes were kept out of a forty-mile zone from the launchpad. Offshore boats were banned for miles.

Vigilant security forces noticed that two small private planes had broken the rules. They were too close to the launchpad. They were forced to land. Officials questioned the pilots for a long time. Finally, NASA officials were satisfied that the pilots had made an innocent mistake and set them free.

With security out of the way, *Atlantis* blasted off at 3:44 P.M., on April 8, 2002. STS-110 was commanded by Lieutenant Colonel Michael Bloomfield and piloted by Lieutenant Commander Stephen Frick. Ellen Ochoa was one of five mission specialists. She was once again going to use the robotic arm. This time it was a Canadian-built robotic arm called *Canadarm*. It had three joints: shoulder, elbow, and wrist. The *rom Canadarm* weighed 905 pounds (410 kilograms). It was strong enough to lift something weighing 585,000 pounds (266,000 kilograms). The truss they were going to install weighed

27,000 pounds. It would have to be carefully lifted from the cargo bay and attached to the *Destiny* module.

Ellen Ochoa was really looking forward to reaching the International Space Station and docking. The last time she and her crewmates had traveled through space to the ISS, it was much smaller. More importantly, there was no crew living there. Now, a crew waited to meet

Ellen Ochoa looks through the earth observation window in the *Destiny* laboratory on the International Space Station (ISS). Portions of the space shuttle *Atlantis* and the *rom Canadarm2* are visible through the window.

"I can only imagine the amazement and pride my grandparents would feel, having been born in Mexico in the 1870s, on knowing that their granddaughter grew up to travel in space."[2]–Ellen Ochoa reflecting on her astronaut career.

them. Ochoa said, "They will greet us once we get there." Ochoa and the *Atlantis* crew brought special foods and music to share with the ISS crew. Ochoa said they were "looking forward to sitting down together and swapping stories."[3] The *Atlantis* crew brought Texas barbecued beef, mashed potatoes, and corn. The crew on the ISS prepared special Russian and Japanese foods for their dinner together. When the *Atlantis* docked with the ISS, the two crews sampled one another's food and had a friendly exchange. The ISS astronauts welcomed visitors from the earth as much as Ellen Ochoa and her crewmates delighted in finding a crew living on the space station.

When the moment came to remove the truss from the cargo bay of the shuttle, there was concern. The *Canadarm* had malfunctioned during an earlier test. One of the joints had not worked. New software was added. Now Ochoa delicately maneuvered the robotic arm to lift the truss from the cargo bay. Everybody was relieved to see it coming out smoothly. Next Ochoa maneuvered the truss into position on the *Destiny* science module. She eased it into position. When it was at the right spot, a temporary clasp grabbed it. Later, space-walking astronauts from the *Atlantis* would attach the truss to the science module with permanent bolts. Everything worked perfectly. But now the tough work began. The robotic arm would be used to maneuver the space walkers around the station to bolt the truss down and hook it up to the ISS.

Steven Smith and Rex Walheim were the space walkers. They carried V-shaped struts to bolt the truss down. The space walk lasted eight hours. As Walheim put the last twist on the bolt, he shouted, "Hot dog!"[4] Mission Control told Ellen Ochoa and her partner Daniel Bursch, "You set a new world record" for operating the robotic arm.[5]

In addition to attaching the truss, the astronauts also installed a $190 million track. Rail cars would move along the framework, taking cargo from one end to the other. Called the Mobile Transporter, it runs on twin rails. It moves at a speed of one inch per second. Hooking up the rail system was the last job the space walkers performed on this mission.

Atlantis landed at 12:27 P.M. on April 19, 2002, at Kennedy Space Center under brilliant blue skies. NASA radioed from Houston, "That was a great landing and a great way to end a mission that has been superb in all respects."[6]

Ellen Ochoa was named deputy director of flight crew operations at Johnson Space Center, and she was eager to continue her work in the space program. She said she planned to work at NASA for "quite a number of years and beyond that I'll have to wait and see what I will do."[7]

Ellen Ochoa was asked to choose one experience that stood out most clearly from her last flight. She said, "I have a lingering memory from my last flight. The sun set shortly after we undocked from the space station." As they were moving away from the ISS, the crew saw the southern lights. They were ghostly green filaments stretching endlessly into space, with bursts of color at their tips. "This beautiful, eerie sight mesmerized the crew," Ochoa said. "Suddenly, it was sunrise, and the whole station turned a brilliant white. It was an incredible moment."[8]

Ellen Ochoa then added, "Working so closely with a team to accomplish a challenging, meaningful task is the greatest reward of being an astronaut."[9]

In June 2002, Ellen Ochoa addressed students entering Phi Beta Kappa, the honor society she belonged to. Now a trustee at Stanford University, she urged the students to let their minds and hearts be their guides in choosing a career and working at it. "If you're not having fun, you're not doing it right," she said. She told them

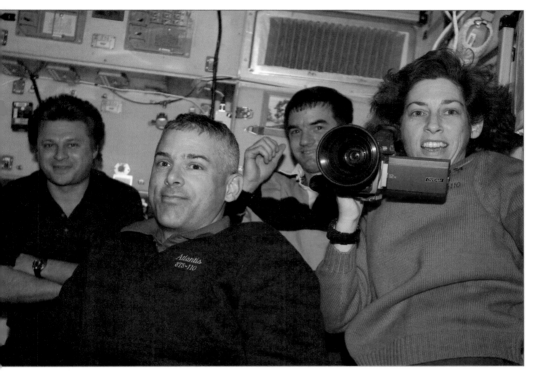

Astronauts Lee M. E. Morin (left foreground), Ellen Ochoa, cosmonaut Yury I. Onufrienko (left background), Expedition Four mission commander, and astronaut Rex J. Walheim, STS-IIO mission specialist, are photographed in the Zvezda Service Module on the International Space Station (ISS).

not to get bogged down in endless meetings and paperwork. She said if they do that, they will "*not* be having fun."[10] Ochoa told the students about the wonderful experiences she had on her space missions and said, "I could wish nothing better for you than the opportunity for such an experience."[11]

Ellen Ochoa began speaking to young people after she first became an astronaut. She especially enjoyed encouraging Latino children. Now she had more time to do something she enjoyed and felt was worthwhile. During her four space flights, she had logged 978 hours on her missions. Now she had another mission—she headed for the classrooms of America with more enthusiasm than ever.

Ellen Ochoa would throw out a challenge to young audiences: "How far do you want your education to take you?"[12] She urged them to dream big. Then they should reach as far as their dreams could stretch. Above all, she told them to get as much education as they could.

Ochoa shared with the students her own path in life. She recalled the one teacher who tried to discourage her from taking engineering. The teacher thought it would be too tough for a girl. Ochoa admitted that for a little while that teacher had taken her off her path—the path she was meant to follow. But soon she realized he was wrong, and she got back on track. Ochoa told her audiences how much different her life would have been if she had let those discouraging words guide her life. She told the students to ignore people who say that something cannot be done because you are a girl, or because you are a Latino, or for any reason. She told them to follow their own star.

Ellen Ochoa spoke to many school assemblies. Students were always eager to meet someone who had been in space. The best part of the assemblies always came when Ellen Ochoa opened the session to questions. A popular question from the children was, how do astronauts sleep in space? How can someone sleep in a weightless state when they are floating around? Ochoa told them about sleeping bags on the space shuttles with hooks attached to them. Once you found a hook to attach to, your sleeping bag floated gently like a hammock in the wind.

Eating in space was a very popular topic. Ellen Ochoa told the students how early astronauts had to squeeze food from a tube. Now they had freeze-dried food in packets. By adding hot water, the food became tasty. Ochoa described the variety of food that can be eaten in space, including nuts, granola, cookies, and dried fruit.

The student listeners enjoyed some funny stories about space from Ellen Ochoa. She told them about sipping hot coffee while flying thousands of miles above the South Seas. She told them of struggling to eat spaghetti in a weightless atmosphere. She also described seeing

Food in Space

Many astronauts have been asked to describe their favorite foods on space missions. The winning list includes shrimp cocktail, chocolate pudding, dried beef, nuts, butter cookies, orange-mango drinks, and granola bars. In space, astronauts prepare their own food. They attach the food tray to a wall bracket. Astronauts each have one set of silverware, including a knife, a fork, and two spoons. They also have a pair of scissors for cutting open their food packets.

**Freeze-dried
Neapolitan ice
cream in a pack.**

sixteen beautiful sunsets in
a single day as the space shuttle
circled the globe.

When asked to describe her scariest moment in space, Ellen Ochoa admitted there had not been any. There had been no narrow escapes on any of her flights.

Many students wanted to know Ochoa's views on the possibility of life on other planets in space. In her view, they wondered, were there aliens out there? Ochoa said there were so many stars in the galaxy that there could be life elsewhere. Was it intelligent life or simple cells? Ellen Ochoa admitted she did not know, and nobody really knew.

In a 2003 celebration of women at the University of Texas, Ochoa spoke to South Texas children. She showed them a video of the space shuttle. They saw Ochoa working and having fun, too. They watched her play the flute and enjoy conversations with fellow astronauts. The young people bonded with her as they always did.

"I'm not trying to make every kid an astronaut," Ellen Ochoa explained. She just wanted them to get a good education and understand how many careers were open to them.[13]

After the successful April mission of *Atlantis*, NASA continued to build the International Space Station piece by piece. In June 2002, STS-111 added a platform to the ISS. In October 2002, *Atlantis* flew again, installing another truss to the framework. In November 2002, still another truss was installed. The final shape of the ISS was slowly but surely forming. The ISS had living space, a science laboratory, storage modules, and solar-power panels. It was getting a stronger backbone with the addition of every truss.

At NASA, Ellen Ochoa was working to help develop new robotic procedures. She also worked in Mission Control, communicating with crews in orbit. One of Ochoa's most important jobs was working with the Russian Federal Space Agency. With American astronauts riding *Soyuz* spacecrafts and crews being traded, close coordination was vital. Everything had to be smooth. Ochoa also worked on NASA's budget and the astronaut training program. She was not in space, but she was still reaching for the stars.

Leading NASA

On January 16, 2003, Ellen Ochoa was working for NASA at Mission Control. NASA was about to launch another space shuttle: *Columbia* STS-107. The commander of this mission was Rick D. Husband. He had been the pilot on Ellen Ochoa's third space flight, and they had become friends. STS-107 was a sixteen-day research mission. The astronauts conducted eighty experiments in the mission. During the mission, all went well and *Columbia* was due for a landing at Kennedy Space Center on February 1.

At 8:52 A.M., on February 1, *Columbia* crossed the coast of California. At 8:54 A.M., the space shuttle passed over eastern California. At that time, the temperature in the left wheel well went up. During the next five minutes, *Columbia*'s left side got dangerously hot. At 8:58 A.M., as the shuttle flew over New Mexico, there was drag on the left side. Shortly after that, communications with the crew of *Columbia* ended. Mission Control tried desperately to regain contact. NASA flight director LeRoy Cain was still hopeful that *Columbia* was all right. There were ominous signs, but Cain continued to think the space shuttle would land safely.

Columbia was crossing the southwestern United States when reports starting from East Texas came in describing debris falling to earth. Cain said, "All we knew was we had a significant event that was potentially catastrophic."[1] But even then, hope remained. Even if the space shuttle was losing pieces, the module containing the seven astronauts might still be saved.

When news reports began to come in indicating that a great deal of debris was falling from the sky, a camera picked up an image of LeRoy Cain's face. He was blinking back tears. No microphone picked up anything that was said in that tragic moment. The photographic evidence of the reaction from NASA officials is all there. The look on the faces of NASA officials tells the story. Phil Engelauf, senior flight director, turned to Deputy of Flight Operations Ellen Ochoa. Ochoa shut her eyes while her lips formed the words, "Oh, God."[2]

Losing *Columbia* with seven astronauts aboard was a terrible blow to the NASA family. For Ellen Ochoa, there was a special pain in the death of her personal friend, Rick D. Husband. Just as Ochoa shared in the triumphs of the space program, she now joined in sorrow grieving the crew members of STS-107.

Initial inquiries into the disaster pointed to something that happened when *Columbia* was launched. A chunk of foam insulation fell off the shuttle's fuel tank and hit the wing of the spacecraft. When *Columbia*

Entry flight director LeRoy Cain holds his hand over his face as workers in Mission Control wait for a signal from the space shuttle _Columbia_ crew minutes before the scheduled landing on February I, 2003. The crew aboard the shuttle _Columbia_ perished when it broke up during its return to earth.

reentered to land, the very hot gases associated with reentry got into the shuttle through the damaged wing, causing an explosion and the breakup of *Columbia*.

The space shuttle program was grounded for two and a half years during the inquiry into the disaster. Because of the damage done at launch to *Columbia,* NASA instituted a system of detailed inspection of launches with special attention to any damage inflicted by anything coming loose. Had the crew of *Columbia* known of the damage to the wing, a space-walking astronaut might have been able to make repairs. During the time the space shuttle program was grounded, Russia supplied the ISS and rotated the crews there using their *Soyuz* spacecrafts. It would be July 26, 2003, before another space shuttle was launched by the United States.

In addition to her duties at NASA, Ellen Ochoa continued speaking to students, often about a career in education. "A hallmark of the Latino community is to help one another," she said. "If students are interested in a way to give back and help their communities, becoming a teacher is probably one of the very best ways of doing this."[3]

It was therefore a moment of joy for Ellen Ochoa when two schools were named after her: the Ellen Ochoa Middle School in Pasco, Washington, and the Ellen Ochoa Learning Center in Cudahy, California. The Ellen Ochoa Learning Center enrolls students in kindergarten up to the eighth grade and is predominently Latino. Ochoa attended the naming ceremony in

Cudahy to thank the school for honoring her in such a way. The staff and students at Cudahy chose Ellen Ochoa's name because she was considered a great role model for all children.

At the Ellen Ochoa Middle School in Pasco, there are about eight hundred students. The school opened in 2003 with fifty-four teachers. The idea for picking Ochoa's name at that school came from her speaking tours. People at the school admired how Ochoa urged children to dream big and then work hard to achieve their goals.

In February 2004, the Smithsonian Center opened a special exhibit that began at the National Museum of American History in Washington, D.C. The exhibit traveled all over the country to promote understanding of Latino culture and contributions. Included in the exhibit were photographs and stories of Latino Americans, both famous and little known, who have made important contributions to American life. Ellen Ochoa was featured along with New Mexico governor Bill Richardson, actress Chita Rivera, and Alfred Rascon, who received the Medal of Honor for heroism as an army combat medic during the Vietnam War. Anna Cabral, executive director of the Smithsonian Center for Latino Initiatives, explained, "We are trying to elevate the presence and contributions of Latinos in U.S. history."[4]

On April 9, 2005, Rosanne Ochoa, whom Ellen Ochoa proudly called her "super mentor" as well as mother, died at the age of eighty-four. Ellen Ochoa's successes are known all over the world, but the successes of Rosanne Ochoa's other four children are also a tribute to this remarkable woman. Her influence on all her children was deep and lasting. Her eldest son, Monte, works as a media specialist for San Diego schools. Her eldest daughter, Beth, earned a doctorate from the University of La Verne College of Law. She worked at Universal Studios/MCA as a records composer and arranger. Her work has been part of five hundred movies, television programs, and sound tracks. She was also a lawyer specializing in the entertainment industry until her death on January 24, 2008. Tyler Ochoa is a professor of law at Santa Clara University. Rosanne Ochoa's youngest son, Wilson Ochoa, is a music librarian with the Nashville Symphony in Tennessee.

Rosanne Ochoa's long life was remembered by her grateful children. They felt sadness at losing her, but they also felt joy at the many gifts she shared so generously with her loved ones and her community. They resolved to carry on her passion for education and determination to follow their dreams.

In 2006, Ellen Ochoa became the director of flight crew operations at Johnson Space Center. In February 2007, a serious incident occurred. A shadow was cast over NASA because of the behavior of astronaut Lisa M. Nowak. Before this, there had not been any incident involving alleged misbehavior on the part of NASA astronauts. They had what was called a squeaky-clean image. This made the incident all the more troubling.

Lisa M. Nowak was arrested for allegedly attacking Air Force Captain Colleen Shipman with pepper spray. The two women were supposedly rivals for the affection of astronaut Commander William A. Oefelein. The incident raised questions of stress among the astronauts based on long absences from their family. NASA removed Nowak from duty and later discharged her. But people were asking whether NASA was taking good enough care of the astronauts and their families.

In the summer of 2007, another disturbing problem arose. Accusations were made about alcohol use among the astronauts while on the job. One allegation described an astronaut impaired by alcohol who was launched aboard a *Soyuz* spacecraft. NASA forbids astronauts from drinking alcoholic beverages twelve hours before a flight. It is called the twelve-hour bottle-to-throttle rule.

Ellen Ochoa, speaking on behalf of NASA, said, "It's an inescapable fact that human spaceflight involves humans. It's complex in making sure that we train people—both on the ground and in orbit to carry out their tasks—to understand that everybody's human."[5]

Many astronauts expressed shock and disbelief at the allegations. They said they never saw instances of alcohol use on the job. Ellen Ochoa agreed. She said she had been with NASA for seventeen years, and she never saw anyone who was impaired by alcohol on the job. She said that the stories that were circulating about widespread drinking at NASA were "events that baffle us."[6]

> **"We're going to be asking ourselves, 'Is there more that we should be doing postflight?'"**
> **–Ellen Ochoa comments on astronaut stress and the mental health of astronauts.[7]**

Still, the allegations grabbed the attention of Congress. Though no solid evidence was ever provided to prove the allegations, Representative Bart Gordon of Tennessee, chairperson of the Committee on Science and Technology, issued a stern statement. "Drinking and driving is never a good idea—least of all when the vehicle involved is a multibillion dollar space shuttle or a high performance jet aircraft."[8]

The Subcommittee on Space and Aeronautics of the United States House of Representatives was concerned enough to ask for NASA to send someone to talk to them about the issue. On September 6, 2007, Ellen Ochoa appeared before the committee. She assured the committee that every day, astronauts are expected to be at their peak, "both mentally and physically." She compared the rigors of training at NASA to practicing for the Olympic Games.[9]

Ellen Ochoa

Ellen Ochoa answers questions during a news conference to discuss the findings of two reviews regarding astronaut medical and behavioral health assessments at NASA Headquarters in Washington on July 27, 2007.

Ellen Ochoa described at length how the space agency makes sure the astronauts are fit for duty. Before astronauts launch into space, NASA tests and interviews them. Ochoa said the astronauts are under constant watch. On the days before a launch, NASA officials pay special attention to the astronauts' health. The officials at NASA want to make sure the men and women who fly into space are not a risk to themselves or to their crewmates. Ochoa then said that following the Lisa M. Nowak incident, NASA would give more attention to looking for signs of stress. She said officials would note changes in behavior.

Ellen Ochoa assured the committee that she never personally saw any evidence of alcohol use among her fellow astronauts. She discussed investigations under way to make the no-drinking rule even more strict. She said meetings were being held with astronauts and their families and flight surgeons to find better ways of making sure astronauts are ready for their mission.

Ellen Ochoa promised the committee that she would do all that she could to get to the bottom of any problems in the astronaut corps. Then she made a heartfelt statement. "I admire and respect what America's astronauts accomplish day in and day out," she said. She pointed to the great success in assembling the International Space Station. "We are able to accomplish these extraordinary feats because of the extraordinary people at NASA, our engineers, flight controllers, scientists, doctors, and our astronauts."[10]

In the summer of 2007, NASA chose the Ellen Ochoa Learning Center in Cudahy, California, as one of twenty-five schools to be partners in the Explorer program. NASA designed the program to attract students to the science, technology, engineering, and mathematics fields. NASA's Jet Propulsion Laboratory in Pasadena, California, would manage the program. Ochoa was happy that her namesake school would be part of this important drive to interest American children in these vital fields.

On September 17, 2007, NASA chose Ellen Ochoa to become the next deputy director at Johnson Space Center. She would succeed Bob Cabana. Director Mike Coats at NASA spoke of Ochoa in glowing terms. "Ellen has proven her exceptional capabilities many times in space as well as in her many roles on the ground, including most recently, her superb management of flight crew operations," he said. "We are extremely fortunate to bring her outstanding reputation throughout the agency and her wealth of experience to this new task."[11]

Ellen Ochoa assumed her new duties after the November 2007 completion of space shuttle mission STS-120.

As Ellen Ochoa serves at Johnson Space Center, she will be responsible for the day-to-day management of the shuttle program. The space shuttle program is the main activity at NASA. Ochoa will establish policy and decide with advisors how the program goes forward. But ever-present in her heart and mind will be her other role—a role very dear to her heart. She knows she is a role model to the younger generation. She knows how important children are to the future of the space program.

Long before she became a veteran space shuttle astronaut, Ellen Ochoa recalled a day in San Francisco. She had just become the first Latina astronaut at NASA. She was sharing her excitement with a group of children at a Catholic school. One Latino boy listened attentively. When she was done speaking, he joined the group of children who surrounded Ellen Ochoa. "I'm glad you came," he said. "You've inspired us."[12]

A Beautiful Moment for NASA

STS-120 was launched on October 23, 2007, with space shuttle *Discovery* commanded by Pamela Melroy. She was only the second woman at NASA to command a space shuttle mission. Upon docking with the International Space Station, Melroy was welcomed by space station commander Peggy Whitson. The mission turned out to be challenging. The space station's solar panel array had been damaged. It had to be repaired if the mission was to be successful.

Scott Parazynski, who had been a mission specialist on STS-66 with Ellen Ochoa, made a daring space walk to make the repair. Riding on the end of a ninety-foot robotic arm, he worked for two hours. He cut loose a tangled clump of wires and patched everything up. When *Discovery* landed at Kennedy Space Center, Commander Melroy said, "It really was a beautiful moment for NASA. What you saw is who we are at NASA."[13]

Chronology

1958—Ellen Lauri Ochoa born in Los Angeles, California, on May 10.

1959—Moves with family to La Mesa, California.

1975—Graduates from Grossmont High School as valedictorian.

1980—Graduates from San Diego State University with a Bachelor of Science degree in physics.

1981—Receives a Master of Science degree from Stanford University in electrical engineering.

1985—Receives a doctorate from Stanford University in electrical engineering. Works at Sandia National Laboratories.

1987—Receives first of three patents in optical research.

1988—Works at Ames Research Center.

1990—Chosen by National Aeronautics and Space Administration (NASA) for astronaut training. Marries Coe Fulmer Miles.

1991—Completes NASA training. Becomes first Latina astronaut.

1993—First flight into space as mission specialist on STS-56 *Discovery* space shuttle. Operates robotic arm on nine-day mission to study sun and earth atmosphere.

1994—Second flight into space as mission specialist and payload commander on STS-66 *Atlantis* space shuttle. Operates robotic arm on eleven-day mission for further study of atmosphere.

1995–1998—Becomes mother of two sons, Wilson and Jordan.

1999—Third flight on STS-96 *Discovery* space shuttle. Docking with International Space Station to load supplies.

2002—Fourth flight aboard STS-110 *Atlantis* space shuttle to build more structures at the ISS. Named deputy director of flight crew operations at Johnson Space Center.

2006—Becomes director of flight crew operations at Johnson Space Center.

2007—Becomes deputy director at Johnson Space Center.

Chapter Notes

CHAPTER 1. SPACE ADVENTURE

1. Memo Munoz, "1st Latina in Space Is Ready for the 2nd Trip," *Los Angeles Times,* May 27, 1993, p. 1.

2. "Astronauts Orbit Spacecraft for Two Days of Solar Study," *Washington Post,* April 12, 1993, p. A09.

3. "Shuttle Crew Releases Craft to Study Solar Winds," *New York Times,* April 12, 1993, p. B10.

4. Mary Anne Perez, "City Terrace Latina Astronaut Clarifies the Mission," *Los Angeles Times,* May 30, 1993, p. 11.

5. "Astronauts Snag Solar Data Satellite They Had Freed," *Los Angeles Times,* April 14, 1993, p. 12.

6. Munoz, p.1.

CHAPTER 2. CALIFORNIA CHILDHOOD

1. Jack Williams, "Rosanne Ochoa, 84; Graduated From SDSU 22 Years After Start," *San Diego Union-Tribune,* April 15, 2005, p. B5.

2. Ibid.

3. Megan Sullivan, "An Interview With NASA Astronaut Ellen Ochoa," *Science Teacher,* February 2005, pp. 60–61.

4. Williams, p. B5.

CHAPTER 3. EDUCATION

1. Dr. Ellen Ochoa, "Education . . . The Stepping Stone to the Stars," *La Prensa San Diego,* December 7, 2001.

2. Ibid.

3. "Star-Trekking: Ellen Ochoa, Ph.D.," *WomenWorking.com,* September 2006, <http://www.womenworking.com/feature/index.php?id-87> (November 2007).

4. Diane Telgen and Jim Kamp, eds., *Latinas! Women of Achievement* (New York: Visible Ink Press, 1996), p. 283.

5. "Ellen Ochoa, Ph.D.: A Higher Education," *Stanford University School of Engineering Annual Report, 1997–98,* <http://soe.stanford.edu/about/AR97-98/ochoa.html> (November 2007).

CHAPTER 4. INVENTOR

1. "Preflight Interview: Ellen Ochoa," *Las Culturas,* May 28, 1999, <http://www.lasculturas.com/lib/sd/blsd052899.htm> (November 2007).

2. Diane Telgen and Jim Kamp, eds., *Latinas! Women of Achievement* (New York: Visible Ink Press, 1996), p. 282.

3. Simon Romero, "Bell Gardens 1st Latina Astronaut Visits High School," *Los Angeles Times,* December 18, 1994, p. 6.

4. Telgen and Kamp, p. 281.

Chapter 5. Training to Be an Astronaut

1. "Ellen Ochoa," *Gale Cengage Learning,* Hispanic Heritage, <http://www.gale.cengage.com/free_resources/chh/bio/ochoa_e.htm> (November 2007).

2. "An Interview With NASA Astronaut Ellen Ochoa," *Science Teacher,* February 2005, pp. 60–61.

3. "Ellen Ochoa, Ph.D.: A Higher Education," *Stanford University School of Engineering Annual Report, 1997–98,* <http://soe.stanford.edu/about/AR97-98/ochoa.html> (November 2007).

4. Michael Bunch, "NASA-like Lab Offers Wonders of Universe," *San Diego Union,* January 23, 1992, p. B.2.5.6.

5. Anne Hart, "Without Limits," *Graduating Engineer Online,* <http://www.graduatingengineer.com/articles/19991112/Without-Limits> (November 2007).

6. Memo Munoz, "1st Latina in Space Is Ready for 2nd Trip," *Los Angeles Times,* May 27, 1993, p. 1.

7. David Graham, "La Mesa Astronaut Set to Soar," *San Diego Union-Tribune,* April 5, 1993, p. B1.

Chapter 6. The First Flight

1. Diane Telgen and Jim Kamp, eds., *Latinas! Women of Achievement* (New York: Visible Ink Press, 1996), p. 284.

2. "Atlantis Shuttle Mission STS-56," *Smithsonian Institution,* <http://www.smithsonianeducation.org/scitech/impacto/graphic/ellen/atlantis_sts56.html> (November 2007).

3. Memo Munoz, "1st Latina in Space Is Ready for 2nd Trip," *Los Angeles Times,* May 27, 1993, p. 1.

4. Jeff Ristine, "Pursue Dreams, Ochoa Urges Kids," *San Diego Union-Tribune,* May 12, 1993, p. A1.

5. Leonel Sanchez, "Astronaut Gives Wings to Pupils' Dreams," *San Diego Union-Tribune,* September 10, 1993, p. B2.

6. Lillian Salazar Leopold, "This Time Lot Less Space Between Ochoa, Class," *San Diego Union-Tribune,* May 13, 1993, p. B.3.1.5.

7. Ibid.

8. Ibid.

9. Mary Anne Perez, "City Terrace Latina Astronaut Clarifies the Mission," *Los Angeles Times,* May 30, 1993, p. 11.

10. Ibid.

11. Sanchez, p. B2.

12. Ibid.

13. Ristine, p. A1.

14. "Ellen Ochoa," *Gale Cengage Learning,* Hispanic Heritage, <http://www.gale.cengage.com/free_resources/chh/bio/ochoa_e.htm> (November 2007).

15. Sanchez, p. B2.

16. Ibid.

CHAPTER 7. PAYLOAD COMMANDER

1. John Noble Wilford, "6 Astronauts Are Launched Into Space," *New York Times,* November 4, 1994, p. A27.

2. "Atlantis Shuttle Mission STS-66," *Smithsonian Institution,* <http://www.smithsonianeducation.org/scitech/impacto/graphic/ellen/atlantis_sts56.html> (October 2007).

3. Anne Hart, "Without Limits," *Graduating Engineer Online,* <http://www.graduatingengineer.com/articles/19991112/Without-Limits> (November 2007).

4. "STS-66," NASA Space Shuttle Launch Archive, <http://science.ksc.nasa.gov/shuttle/missions/sts-66/mission-sts-66.html> (November 2007).

5. Ibid., p. 24.

6. Ibid.

7. "Shuttle Atlantis Crew Retrieves Satellite Measuring Ozone Layer," *Los Angeles Times,* November 13, 1994, p. 16.

8. Ibid.

9. "STS-66," p. 28.

10. "Shuttle Atlantis Crew Retrieves Satellite," p. 16.

11. "STS-66," pp. 29–30.

12. Ibid., p. 37.

CHAPTER 8. INTERNATIONAL SPACE STATION

1. "Star-Trekking: Ellen Ochoa, Ph.D.," *WomenWorking.com,* September 2006, <http://www.womenworking.com/feature/index.php?id-87> (November 2007).

2. Angela Posada-Swafford, "A Place in the Stars," *Hispanic Magazine,* June 2003, p. 1.

3. "Preflight Interview: Ellen Ochoa," *Las Culturas,* May 28, 1999, <http://www.lasculturas.com/lib/sd/blsd052899a.htm> (November 2007).

4. "Preflight Interview: Ellen Ochoa," *National Aeronautics and Space Administration,* <http://spaceflight.nasa.gov/shuttle/archives/sts-110/crew/intochoa.html> (November 2007).

5. William Harwood, "Structural Truss Added to Spine of Space Station," *Washington Post,* October 15, 2000, p. A03.

6. Ibid.

7. Cheryl Walker, "Woman Reaches Her Dream," *San Diego Union-Tribune,* May 28, 2000, p. B2.

8. Ibid.

Chapter 9. Fourth Space Flight and Beyond

1. Warren E. Leary, "Shuttle Crew Plans to Give Space Station Its First Rail Link, *New York Times,* April 2, 2002, p. F2.

2. "Meet NASA Astronaut Ellen Ochoa," *Girl Power Guests,* <http://www.girlpower.gov/girlarea/gpguests/ochoa.htm> (November 2007).

3. "Preflight Interview: Ellen Ochoa," *Las Culturas,* May 28, 1999, <http://www.lasculturas.com/lib/sd/blsd052899a.htm> (November 2007).

4. "Astronauts, for Starters, Bolt a Girder to Station," *Los Angeles Times,* April 12, 2002, p. A34.

5. Ibid.

6. "Shuttle Glides Home After Ambitious Mission," *New York Times,* April 20, 2002, p. A13.

7. Diane Telgen and Jim Kamp, eds., *Latinas! Women of Achievement* (New York: Visible Ink Press, 1996), p. 284.

8. Megan Sullivan, "An Interview With NASA Astronaut Ellen Ochoa," *Science Teacher,* February 2005, pp. 60–61.

9. Ibid.

10. Dawn Levy, "Stay Cool Under Pressure, Astronaut Ellen Ochoa Tells Phi Beta Kappa Inductees," *Stanford Report,* June 19, 2002, p. 1.

11. Ibid., p. 2.

12. Anne Hart, "Without Limits," *Graduating Engineer Online,* <http://www.graduatingengineer.com/articles/19991112/Without-Limits> (November 2007).

13. "Ellen Ochoa, Ph.D.: A Higher Education," *Stanford University School of Engineering Annual Report, 1997–98,* <http://soe.stanford.edu/about/AR97-98/ochoa.html> (November 2007).

CHAPTER 10. LEADING NASA

1. John Schwartz, "NASA Official Says He Held Out Hope in Final Moments," *New York Times,* February 15, 2003, p. A1.

2. Ibid.

3. "Dr. Ellen Ochoa: Education . . . The Stepping Stone to the Stars," *La Prensa San Diego,* December 7, 2001.

4. Sylvia Morena, "Latino Achievers in Smithsonian Spotlight," *Washington Post,* February 18, 2004, p. B03.

5. Peter N. Spotts, "Astronauts Fly When Unfit for Duty," *Christian Science Monitor,* July 30, 2007, p. 3.

6. Marc Kaufman, "NASA Knew About Preflight Drinking Among Astronauts," *Washington Post,* July 28, 2007, p. A1.

7. John Schwartz, et al., "For Astronauts and Their Families, Lives With Built-In Stress," *New York Times,* February 9, 2007, p. A15.

8. Kaufman, p. A1.

9. Statement of Ellen Ochoa, Ph.D., before the Subcommittee on Science and Technology of the United States House of Representatives, September 6, 2007, p. 1.

10. Ibid., p. 5.

11. "NASA Names Astronaut Ellen Ochoa Deputy Director of Johnson," NASA, <http://www.prnewswire.com/egi-bin/stories.pl?ACCT=104&STORY=www/story/09-17> (November 2007).

12. Diane Telgen and Jim Kamp, eds., *Latinas! Women of Achievement* (New York: Visible Ink Press, 1996), p. 284.

13. "Welcome Back Astronauts," *International Space Station Stuff,* November 8, 2007, <http://iss-stuff.blogspot.com/> (October 8, 2008).

Further Reading

Hasday, Judy L. *Ellen Ochoa.* New York: Chelsea House
   Publishers, 2007.

Iverson, Teresa. *Ellen Ochoa.* Chicago: Raintree, 2006.

Paige, Joy. *Ellen Ochoa: The First Hispanic Woman in Space.*
   New York: The Rosen Publishing Group, 2004.

Rodriguez, Robert, and Tamra B. Orr (contributing writers).
   Great Hispanic-Americans. Lincolnwood, Ill. : Publications
   International, ©2005.

Sparrow, Giles (foreword by Buzz Aldrin). *Spaceflight: The
   Complete Story from Sputnik to Shuttle—and Beyond.*
   New York.: DK Pub., 2007.

Internet Addresses

Official Ellen Ochoa biography.
<http://www.jsc.nasa.gov/Bios/htmlbios/ochoa.html>

NASA Missions.
<http://www.nasa.gov/missions/index.html>

Atlantis Shuttle Mission STS-56. Ochoa's first flight.
<http://www.smithsonianeducation.org/scitech/impacto/graphic/ellen/atlantis_sts56.html>

Index